The Disn

Chronicling the M

and the Parks

Aaron H. Goldberg

Published by Quaker Scribe Publishing.
quakerscribe@gmail.com
First printing 2016
ISBN 978-0-692-74281-5

CONTENTS

When Winter Comes. Released May 11, 1924. Reviewed issue May 17, pg. 2364.

Homeless Pups. Released May 4, 1924. Reviewed issue May 17, pg. 2364

An Ideal Farm. Released Apr. 27, 1924. Reviewed issue Apr. 26, pg. 1913.

A Trip To The Pole. Released Apr. 20, 1924. Reviewed issue May 3, pg. 2013.

If Noah Lived Today. Released Apr. 13, 1924. Reviewed issue Apr. 19, pg. 1806.

Running Wild. Released Apr. 6, 1924. Reviewed Issue Apr. 5, pg. 1550.

The Champion. Released Mar. 30, 1924.

From Rags To Riches And Back Again. Released Mar. 23, 1924.

Why Mice Leave Home. Released Mar. 16, 1924. Reviewed issue Mar. 15, pg. 1206.

An All Star Cast. Released Mar. 9, 1924.

. **Herman The Great Mouse.** Released March 2, 1924. Reviewed issue March 1, pg. 996.

ALICE COMEDIES. Produced by Walt Disney. Distributed by M. J. Winkler. Star, Virginia Davis. Director, Walt Disney. Combination of Cartoon and Character. Length, 1 reel.

Alice's Day at Sea. Released, Mar. 1, 1924. Reviewed issue Apr. 26, pg. 1913.

Alice's Spooky Adventure. Released Apr. 1, 1924.

Alice's Wild West Show. Released May 1, 1924.

Alice's Fishy Story. Released June 1, 1924.

Alice, the Dog Catcher. Released July 1, 1924.

Alice, the Peacemaker. Released Aug. 1, 1924.

JIMMY AUBREY COMEDIES. Produced by Standard Cinema Corp. Released by Selznick Dist. Corp. Length, two reels.

The Lunatic. Director Joe Rock. Star Jimmy Aubrey. Released Mar. 1, 1924.

The Mechanic. Director, Joe Rock. Star, Jimmy Aubrey. Released Apr. 1, 1924.

A Ghostly Night. Director, Joe Rock. Star, Jimmy Aubrey Released May 1, 1924.

A Perfect Pest. Director, Joe Rock. Star, Jimmy Aubrey. Released June 1, 1924.

The Box Car Limited. Director, Joe Rock. Star, Jimmy Aubrey. Released July 1, 1924.

The Trouble Maker. Director, Joe Rock. Star, Jimmy Aubrey. Released Aug. 1, 1924.

Pretty Soft. Director, Joe Rock. Star, Jimmy Aubrey. Released Aug. 15, 1924.

Cave Inn Sheik. Director, Joe Rock. Star, Jimmy Aubrey. Released Aug. 30, 1924.

Motion Picture News from October 1924 featuring Walt Disney's early series *Alice Comedies*.

The Film Daily from March 6, 1927. Note the bottom left corner, announcing Oswald the Lucky Rabbit, Walt Disney's creation before Mickey Mouse.

The Film Daily from August 1927, mentioning Oswald the Lucky Rabbit.

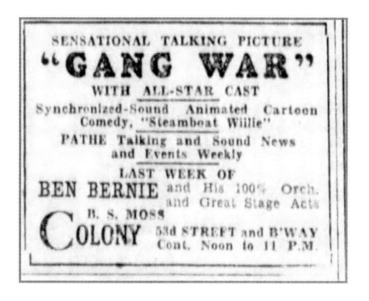

The first advertisement for Mickey Mouse playing at the Colony Theatre in New York City. *The Brooklyn Daily Eagle*, November 28, 1928.

AARON H. GOLDBERG

The Film Daily from January 6, 1929, reviewing *The Gallopin' Gaucho*.

INTRODUCTION

If you're reading this book, chances are you're a fan of some aspect of the Walt Disney Company—be it the theme parks, the movies, or perhaps the company's iconic namesake, Walt Disney. There is also a good chance you're familiar with how the whole Disney "story" got started.

The trials and tribulations of the life that was Walt Disney's before 1928 is a great story, but it's a story that has been told countless times. For the purposes of this book, we are going to bypass those years of Walt's life, from 1901 through 1927, and jump right into the beginning of Mickey's life and, to a large extent, Walt's life in the public eye—and, in turn, our lives with Disney circa 1928 to the present day.

The Disney Story is sort of a two-pronged approach to chronicling Walt, Mickey, and the theme parks. There is the book, which you're holding in your hands, and a more extensive project online at thedisneystory.com, the companion website to the book.

The website follows the book, story for story, decade by decade, in the same chronological order. Instead of my words telling the story, you'll get a chance to read the hundreds of other voices that told the Disney story over the decades, along with the most important voice of all, Walt's.

In the first half of the book, I quote extensively from Walt himself. In every opportunity I could find, I have utilized Walt's own published words to narrate the Disney story, which offers a unique, firsthand perspective.

The media swooned over Walt Disney and his pal Mickey for decades and, by and large, still chronicles every action of the Walt Disney Company. The media did a tremendous job covering Disney, especially during Walt's life. These stories about Disney, released in the media from the 1930s through the 1960s, make for quite an interesting read.

Every direct quote and notable story in the book is followed by an endnote that corresponds to a number on the website where the quoted article can be found in its entirety.

But enough about the website. Let's get back to the book. *The Disney Story* is almost like an abridged biography of the Walt Disney Company. You'll progress chapter by chapter and decade by decade through the events of the company, which obviously encompass stories centered on Walt, Mickey, the movies, the theme parks, and so forth.

Each story starts with a headline and a date marking the debut or opening of that Disney milestone. Following the headline is an informative story or interesting tidbit about this specific milestone. Many of the stories have interesting tertiary facts or side notes, along with some commentary or musings.

There are quite a few stories that aren't your usual, run-of-the-mill milestones—a few are personal to Walt's life, and some are about lesser-known projects or projects that didn't come to fruition or were short-lived—something I like to call "discarded Disney."

I must provide a bit of a disclaimer. As we know, the Disney empire is vast, and everyone's love for Disney is different. While I tried to be complete and touch on the most important and relevant milestones, something you may know and love may not have made the cut. I tried to stick with the major headlines over the decades, with a smattering of lesser-known stories and trivia. Also, a quick note about the dates used to document the milestones in this book: each and every date used came from either the Walt Disney Company's corporate website or from the Disney fan club, D23.

So with that in mind, let the timeline be our tour guide through this fascinating journey. Let's jump right in and begin in the year 1928, when Mickey Mouse made his debut in New York City at the Colony Theatre—the original advertisement from the newspaper the *Brooklyn Daily Eagle*, from Sunday November 18, 1928, can be seen a few pages back.

Aaron H. Goldberg

July 2016

CHAPTER ONE

1930S

November 18, 1928

Steamboat Willie is released, introducing the world to Mickey Mouse, Minnie, and a cartoon fully synchronized with sound.

After Mickey's 1928 debut at the Colony Theatre in New York City, the affable mouse was off and running toward international icon status. Mickey Mouse wasn't the first popular cartoon to take the country by storm. The silent era of animation had many animated stars, but Walt's novel combination of synchronizing animation with sound was winning over theatergoers around the world.

By August of 1929, Mickey was almost a year old and was a rising star in this exciting new domain. Becoming a cultural icon wasn't an easy task. It took a bit of hard work, some creativity, and, for this big screen sensation, a visionary named Walter Elias Disney as his chaperone.

So how did this audible and animated magic happen? An article from August 11, 1929, in the *LA Times*, answers this question and gives a peek behind the curtain at the upstart Disney studio. As the article explains, the studio consisted of eight artists, a musician, and various technical assistants in a building described as a small, one-story, friendly-appearing stucco building at 2719 Hyperion Avenue.[1]

When this article was released, Mickey was set to make his on-screen singing debut, and Walt and his boys at the studio had put lots of time and effort into making Mickey musical.

> "Perhaps Mickey's voice will ring out clear and true for the total time space of one minute." Walt Disney, Mickey's fond creator, conveys the astounding piece of information that

700 drawings will be required to reveal that contraction and expansion of Mickey's throat in the simple act of getting the song out of his system.

These muscular movements of the throat and body must occur in such a fashion that they synchronize perfectly with the notes and words of the theme song, projected of course by a human voice double.

"Just a matter of rhythmics and mathematics," explains Mr. Disney glibly. "In fact, you write the music to fit the drawings and then draw the drawings to fit the music.

"Animated drawings, as it may or may not be known, are simply a series of black and white sketches, one sketch to each different posture or movement of the stiff-legged characters. A cartoon may run five to six minutes. It may contain five to six thousand drawings projected at such a speed that the whole seems a piece of continuous action as if from humans."[1]

Several thousand drawings for one animated short certainly was a time-consuming and laborious task. Thus, with the labor of love known as Mickey Mouse, surely there was no time for another endeavor, correct? Well, Mickey's boom in popularity afforded Walt the opportunity to branch out into another series, the *Silly Symphonies*.

August 22, 1929

The Skeleton Dance is released, the first of the *Silly Symphonies*.

In August of 1929, the first *Silly Symphony*, *The Skeleton Dance*, premiered. The title of the cartoon is a pretty good representation of its subject. According to the *LA Times*, when the short debuted at the Carthay Circle Theatre, it was very well received.

The Skeleton Dance proved a sensational success, taking about as much applause on the occasion of the premiere as the feature itself. The film depicted grotesque skeleton characters dancing weirdly to music of a symphonic—at times nature.[1]

The *Silly Symphonies* do not feature Mickey Mouse or, for that matter, characters that appear episodically. Instead, each one often features a unique story line and character. This series became a vehicle for Walt to create and experiment with new animation techniques and technology, and it became a way to introduce new characters unrelated to Mickey. Many fan favorites made their debuts in this award-winning series.

In 1994, animation historian Jerry Beck released his book *The 50 Greatest Cartoons: As Selected by 1,000 Animation Professionals*, which ranked *The Skeleton Dance* as the eighteenth-best cartoon of all time.

A year and a half after the review of the cartoon in the *LA Times*, *The Skeleton Dance* made its way to Denmark. However, the reception there was a little different—the country's film censor was none too pleased with its creative content.

The Danish film censor "insists that the Danish public must not be allowed to see one of Mr. Disney's *Silly Symphony* films which show dancing skeletons and ghosts in a graveyard. The topic, in the censor's opinion, is too macabre to put on the screen."[2]

July 30, 1932

The Academy Award–winning cartoon *Flowers and Trees* is released, Disney's first full-color cartoon.

On July 30, 1932, Disney released their first full-color cartoon, *Flowers and Trees*, under the *Silly Symphony* franchise. Roughly a month after its debut, the studio announced that during the 1932–1933 season, thirteen more *Silly Symphonies* would be released in Technicolor. Also, the public would be able to enjoy eighteen more Mickey Mouse cartoons.[3]

Although Mickey was still toiling away in black-and-white, the studio promised if the Technicolor cartoons proved successful, Mickey too would meet the same destiny.[3]

Flowers and Trees was indeed successful. In fact, it went on to win the Academy Award for the best animated short film in 1932. The success of the film obviously had a profound impact not only on Disney, but also on the genre itself.

As an interesting side note, in the October 17, 1933, issue of the Hollywood trade paper *Variety*, there is a quick blurb about a little film about to go into production with a *Silly Symphony* influence:

Favorable public reaction to Disney's *Silly Symphonies* has prompted Sam Goldwyn to plan production of *Wizard of Oz* in Technicolor.[4]

November 15, 1932

The Disney Studio forms an art school to train animators.

By November of 1932, Mickey Mouse was four years old, and what a four years it had been. Here are a few statistics for you about Mickey from around his fourth birthday. More than fifteen thousand theaters around the world had shown Mickey Mouse cartoons. Exactly 172 newspapers in the United States ran a Mickey Mouse comic strip daily. Nearly one million children were members of approximately one thousand Mickey Mouse clubs and met every Saturday morning.[5]

More than sixty manufacturers in the United States and Europe made Mickey Mouse dolls, toys, and other knickknacks, which sold in an estimated three hundred thousand retail stores across the globe.[5] Pretty impressive stuff!

From these statistics, we can see the studio was obviously bustling with activity, topping 250 employees working to spread the gospel of Mickey Mouse. Walt needed employees to keep up with the public's demand, yet not just anyone would make the cut.[6]

Many of the workers at the studio had previously worked as newspaper cartoonists, while others were self-taught. Regardless of their backgrounds, however, Walt had stringent standards for those wishing to join his studio.

In the May 1934 issue of *Rotarian* magazine, Walt is quoted about his art school:

> The course takes about six weeks, and when a man finishes,
> I know whether he has the qualifications I need. Only about
> one man in ten has them, and graduates into a steady job.

Another article from March of 1936 illustrated Walt's difficulties in hiring artists he felt were qualified to work at his studio:

> "I need artists—real artists—to train," he says. Disney's
> studio advertised up and down the Pacific Coast for artists,
> received 1,700 replies. Fifty applicants were deemed worthy

of try-outs. Of the 50 only one is still on the Disney staff of approximately 300.

"It takes a real artist," specified Disney, "to fill the bill. A special kind of artist. Many good artists are not fitted for this work. We want men whom we can train to be animators."[7]

December 18, 1933

Walt and Lillian Disney welcome their first child, Diane.

On December 18, 1933, Walt was being honored in Hollywood. He was being awarded a medal for distinguished service to childhood for his creation of Mickey Mouse. However, in the midst of the ceremony, Walt had to leave unexpectedly.

He quickly left the building and rushed over to the hospital, as his wife, Lillian, had just given birth to their daughter, Diane Marie Disney (December 18, 1933–November 19, 2013).[8]

June 9, 1934

Welcome to the Disney family, Donald Duck!

Here we are, in the summer of 1934. The past six years or so have been busy for Walt. Mickey debuted, Walt's daughter was born, and here comes another member of the Disney brood, courtesy of the *Silly Symphonies*.

The Wise Little Hen was released on June 9, 1934. This Technicolor cartoon was based on the fable of the Little Red Hen. The cartoon introduced two new Disney characters, Peter Pig and everyone's favorite curmudgeon, Donald Duck.[9]

February 23, 1935

The first Mickey Mouse cartoon in color is released: *The Band Concert*.

As Walt teased in the article for *Flowers and Trees* in 1932, Mickey finally graduated to color in early 1935 with the release of *The Band Concert*.

So why did it take so long to see Mickey in Technicolor? Well, it appears Walt had his reservations about coloring Mickey. In the February 1935 issue of

Screenland magazine, Walt spoke about Mickey Mouse taking the plunge into living color:

> Now Mickey is about to take a new step. Starting this month, the mouse actor is making his appearance in color! Mr. Mouse has graduated from the ordinary black and white films.
>
> Of course, this is an experiment, Disney frankly admits that his experiment is daring. The public may not like Mickey in his new array of brilliant colors. For that reason, only a few of the cartoon comedies starring the mouse actor will be produced this new way. Then Disney will await the public response. If that response is favorable, Mickey will keep his "coat of colors." If not, Mickey will be returned to his old black and white formula.[10]

Wow. Interesting little blurb there. Despite the enormous success of the *Silly Symphonies*, it's fascinating to see that the studio thought there was a real chance that colorized Mickey could fail and was hesitant to move forward!

As we know, Mickey in color was embraced by his audience. The public wanted more colorful Mickeys and wanted to learn the process Disney used to not only draw him but create him in vibrant, living color.

Numerous articles of the day routinely described the process Disney used to create their cartoons and submerge them into color via the Technicolor process. Here is a brief overview from *Screenland* magazine describing how a Mickey Mouse cartoon from yesterday came to be.

The production process went through several channels to create one Mickey Mouse cartoon. First, the story line came from the scenario department, where the basis of the cartoon was created. Then, once a premise was agreed upon and outlined, the plot took a trip over to the "gag department," where funny situations were created and inserted into the plot.

Once this was completed, the final script was written in two parts. One part went to the animation/photography department. The second went to the sound department. Photography and sound couldn't be done simultaneously, since the photography was done one frame at a time. Therefore, it was necessary first to complete the photography and later to synchronize the sound to fit the actions of the characters.

As you can imagine, actual production was a slow, tedious process. Approximately two weeks were required to photograph a picture that was seen in roughly seven minutes. Some of the most tedious work was not the multitudinous drawings of Mickey--animators had to draw from twelve to sixteen thousand separate characters--but the cameraman's duties. He photographed the cartoon comedies one frame at a time—twelve to sixteen thousand separate, slight turns of the camera crank.

Each drawing of Mickey, as seen on a screen, consists of two drawings. One is of Mickey himself; the other is of the setting in which the mouse appears. For example, if a scene shows Mickey dancing on a table in a cabaret, the drawing of the cabaret and its furnishings was done on white cardboard. The series of drawings of Mickey, showing the various positions of his dance, were done on transparent celluloid.

Thus, to photograph Mickey Mouse dancing in a cabaret, the cameraman had to place the transparent celluloid drawings, one at a time, on top of the cardboard sketch of the cabaret. The effect is that Mickey is actually in the cabaret.

In this sense, there is no motion since each pose is only a black-and-white drawing. But when a series of still photographs, each depicting a slightly advanced pose toward an ultimate active move, are shown in rapid succession, the illusion of motion is attained.

Therefore, motion in animated cartoons is an optical illusion; drawing out the action pose by pose attains it. Sixteen such poses are necessary for each foot of motion picture film.

Walt gave some insight into how the animators may cheat here and there:

> Here is a little trade secret that I reveal for the first time: Many drawings of Mickey Mouse on celluloid are preserved in files. For example, one file is that of Mickey running from left to right across the screen. Tonight, you may see a cartoon comedy in which the mouse runs from left to right across the room. Next week you may see another picture where the mouse runs from left to right across a tennis court. Actually, only the setting may be changed, and by "setting," I mean the cardboard drawings that are placed behind the celluloid series of drawings showing Mickey in the act of running.

Now that the animation is completed, how did Mickey become a "talkie"? Walt revealed he was the voice of Mickey and gave further details into how the studio matched sound with animation.

> There are two ways of synchronizing sound for the cartoon comedies. The most common is to have the various sound technicians watch the cartoon on a screen and to fit noises, voices and music to action.
>
> The more accurate method is the use of the second script, called the "sound script." This method injects sound by the "time process." At a certain, exact second of the sound script, the proper voice or sound or music is recorded. The time is done in this way: There are sixteen separate drawings to each foot of film, so a metronome is set to beat sixteen strokes to the exact number of seconds required to project one foot of film.
>
> Thus, when the sound script indicates that on the tenth drawing of the 456th foot in the picture, Mickey is to speak the words "Hello Minnie" the voice dubber who is to utter that line knows exactly when to speak it—on the tenth beat of the metronome during the 456th foot of film.[10]

Lastly, how did all of that illustrious Technicolor magic happen? This information comes from an article titled "How THREE Color Movies Are Made," from the July 1935 issue of *Modern Mechanix.*

> In photographing a Disney Silly Symphony, three negatives are made, one each for the three colors, red, green, and blue. All colors of the rainbow can be reproduced by a blending of these three primary colors. The three negatives are made through filters which absorb certain portions of the light passing through them. The light striking the red negative is photographed through a red filter that absorbs or stops all the colors except red. This gives a photographic record of the red objects in the picture. In like manner, the green and blue negatives are photographed through green and blue filters.
>
> Walt Disney and his staff paint the cartoons in the colors desired, and then a special Technicolor camera photographs

the three negatives at one operation. The three negatives are made simultaneously through the use of a special prism. Each of these negatives records the intensity and extent of only one color; for instance, on the blue negative is a picture of only the blue color in the objects, on the red negative is the image of the red objects, etc. From each of the three negatives is made a print on a special gelatine coated stock, which is called a "matrix." In making the "matrix," a silver image is not used as in the case of ordinary black and white photography. Instead, a photographic emulsion in the form of a gelatine, sensitive to light, is used.

This gelatine emulsion has the characteristic of hardening under the action of light. When light strikes this emulsion after going through the negative, it becomes hard and insoluble in proportion to the intensity of the light striking it.

In making the red "matrix," a light beam is passed through the negative of the red record by an optical arrangement to strike the "matrix." This is called "optically" printing the "matrix;" after it is printed the soluble portions, that is, the portions not acted on by light, are dissolved away, leaving a relief image. This relief image is then dyed a blue-green color and pressed into contact with the film, which is to be shown on the screen. In pressing this "matrix" into contact, the dye image is printed in a manner not unlike the method used in printing from type in the printing press. The matrices for the other two colors are made and dyed in the same manner, after which they are also pressed into contact on top of the first image. This results in a picture, which is a combination of the three colors, and is the final film ready to be shown on the theater screen. Once the matrices are prepared, as many three-color films as are desired can be printed.[11]

Believe it or not, these elaborate descriptions about how Disney created their cartoons during the 1930s are the abridged versions. An even better perspective of the ingenuity found in the studio back in the 1930s and 1940s can be seen in the Disney movie *The Reluctant Dragon*. It's a great movie that brings to life these processes and the inner workings of the studio.

December 21, 1937

Snow White and the Seven Dwarfs, Disney's first full-length animated film, premieres at the Carthay Circle Theatre.

In less than a decade, the Disney studio went from upstarts to experts in animation and entertainment. They married sound and animation, sprinkled in some color, and, in November of 1937, they upped the ante by utilizing a multiplane camera in the cartoon *The Old Mill*. The multiplane added depth to the picture by separating background and foreground. The new technology paid off handsomely for Disney, as *The Old Mill* won an Academy Award for best cartoon short.

Winning an Academy Award was wonderful and Walt would go on to win more Oscars than anyone else in Hollywood, but 1937 was special for a different reason.

It was time for Walt and the studio to combine everything they had cultivated during the past ten years and make a full-length animated feature film.

Snow White was Walt's muse for this endeavor. Studio employees worked for years to satisfy their ardent taskmaster, Walt, and he in turn in went into hock and to the bank for the film's production. Much of Hollywood wondered if Walt could actually pull this off, or if the film would finally sink the wunderkind.

According to a newspaper review from the day after the premiere, before the film Walt portrayed the eighth dwarf, Nervous.

> Never had any movie had such a worldwide buildup as his "Snow White and the Seven Dwarfs," which he started to manufacture—and publicize—more than three years ago. He spent $1,500,000 on it and more worry than he cares to recall. Then he went to the Carthay Circle theater last night and bit his nails, waiting for the verdict of the tail-coated and satin-gowned audience.[12]

Well, the nervousness was all for naught. Tinseltown's elite showed up; Myrna Loy, Spencer Tracy, Mary Pickford, and 1,500 others spent $5.50 to view Walt's masterpiece. The rounds of applause and praise when the film concluded definitively confirmed that the audience had gotten their money's worth and loved every minute of Disney's version of this popular fairy tale.[12]

As we know, *Snow White* was an enormous success and is very much a timeless film. Even the accompanying music has delighted and imprinted generation after generation. As for what the film meant to the Disney Studio, in many ways it was the catalyst for all things Disney that we know today. The profits from Snow White left the studio on firm footing and replenished the coffers so Walt could indulge in even more creative endeavors.

One last tangential side story about *Snow White*. The April 5, 1938, edition of the *New York Times* ran a brief story about the film being made into a "talking book" for the blind.

The article explained that the film was the first sound picture to be translated into a talking book for blind audiences, as announced by the American Foundation for the Blind.

The "talking book" was composed of long-playing disks like phonograph records, which were played on a special reading machine. The title of each disk was marked in braille.[13] This concept was decades ahead of its time—and leave it to Disney to be part of it!

November 26,1938

Walt and Roy's mother, Flora, passed away.

On January 2, 1938, the Associated Press ran a national story about the brothers Disney—Walt and Roy, along with their other brothers Raymond and Herbert—purchasing a home for their parents. Elias and Flora Disney relocated to Hollywood from Portland, Oregon, and it was the year of their fiftieth wedding anniversary.[14]

Less than a year later, on November 26, 1938, tragedy struck the Disney family. Elias and Flora were found by their maid unconscious in their bedroom, in the very home their children had purchased for them.

Elias was hospitalized and survived the incident, but, unfortunately, Flora passed away. It was discovered that a faulty hot-water heater pilot light had pumped gas fumes into the home, and she succumbed to them.[15]

Now cue the conspiracy theories as to why so many Disney movies have characters with parental issues!

With the grave exception of the tragic death of Flora Disney, the 1930s were a triumphant decade for the not-yet-forty-year-old Walt. Commercial successes aside, the kid from the Midwest with humble beginnings also had some of his creations hanging in the hallowed halls of Metropolitan Museum of Art in 1939.[16]

And, the year before, the Ivy League had come calling, with both Harvard and Yale bestowing honorary degrees upon him.[17] Those two honors may seem ordinary considering the magnitude of success Walt achieved with the creations of Mickey Mouse, Donald Duck, and the innovative feature Snow White. Walt himself was a star, to be eclipsed only by his own creation, Mickey.

Mickey's face was known and loved around the world, and Disney capitalized on it with hundreds of licensing deals throughout the 1930s. There is even the legendary story of Mickey saving the fate of both a watch company[18] and a toy company[19] after both companies faced receivership and bankruptcy. The mouse saved the day in 1933 and 1935 and brought both companies into the black.

With success around every corner, it was time for Disney to grow again and say good-bye to their Hyperion Studios home and say hello to a new dream factory in Burbank.

The Disney studio moved into a fifty-one-acre state-of-the-art facility in late 1939, and it remains the company's headquarters today. When the studio opened, it was truly remarkable for its time, and Walt was proud of his new facility. It even featured a state-of-the-art air-conditioning system that was unique in its own right. If you're interested in learning more about the studio, thedisneystory.com has a roughly forty-page interview Walt gave to a trade journal around the time the studio relocated, which contains more details.[20]

Things were booming at the studio, but paradise doesn't always last forever, not even in the utopian world of cartoons. The 1930s were coming to a close, and the prosperity from *Snow White* wouldn't last forever. Walt continued to invest in the studio's future with more feature films, but tough times were looming. A world war was raging, and it hovered over the studio for much of the 1940s.

CHAPTER TWO

1940S

February 7, 1940

Pinocchio is released and wins Academy Awards for Best Original Score and Best Song—"When You Wish Upon A Star."

With the success of *Snow White* firmly in the Disney rearview mirror, the studio looked to open the 1940s with a bang from another full-length feature, *Pinocchio*. A few days prior to the film's premiere, ever the great promoter, Walt penned an article for the *New York Times*.

The article provided background information on the studio's second full-length feature, along with details about the advances the studio had made since they had wrapped production of *Snow White*.

Walt spoke at length about how the studio had refined the technical process of creating the full-length feature. He dubbed *Snow White* the "Great Experiment" and vowed to resolve any issues the studio faced in creating their next feature film.

Let's hear it from the man himself:

> During '*Pinocchio*,' improvement in the technique of practically every department was made at the studio. For instance, the story used to be developed by pinning rough action sketches of a sequence on a large board. After the story crew was satisfied with it, the storyboard was moved to the director's room where more changes were always made. Then the boards were carted into a projection room where the sequence director got up in front of the crew and narrated the action, doing all the dialogue himself and explaining the sound effects which were to go into the picture.

When we started 'Pinocchio' we changed this and simplified the whole process. We figured out that after the story crew had a sequence in good shape, each story sketch could be photographed on film. The result then could be run on a small screen in a projection room or on a Moviola machine in a director's room with sound and dialogue track running simultaneously.

I think the greatest improvement at our studio has been made in the special effects. Those who saw Snow White, marveled at the realism of the shadows, the highlights on jewels and on shiny objects—the mists, the dusts, the water. I know the experimentation and work that went into Snow White, the days and nights of plotting and scheming, but for 'Pinocchio' this work was doubled.

For the first time in the field of animation audiences will see, in Pinocchio, the warm glow of a lighted match against a man's face as he lights his pipe. They will see underwater effects that look for all the world like super-special marine photography. They will see the Blue Fairy step from a dazzling brilliance of light. They will see the most tremendous whale ever heard of, swimming through the water, his muscles rippling subtly under his blue-black hide. These things helped put gray hair in the heads of all of us.

In a lighter vein and requiring an entirely different technique is the twinkling of the stars in the sky, the shimmer of which is produced by a series of exposures on one film. The shimmer is not obtainable by any single drawing, but the continuity of all exposures produces the effect.

Important and a technique which gives roundness and dimensions to the characters is a process known as the "blend" at our studio. Two girls were responsible for the development and use of this technique on Snow White. With increased production and the many complex problems involved, the staff has now increased to twelve. It is the job of these girls to see that the cheeks have a natural roundness, the arms given a molded appearance. They must use their judgment, as all the

information they have is that furnished by the layout man—
source of light.[1]

Well, now you know about some of the techniques and advances that contributed to the success of this movie that earned two Academy Awards— one for Best Original Score and the other for Best Song ("When You Wish Upon A Star"). *Pinocchio* cost roughly $2.6 million to produce and kept some 1,350 studio employees busy during its production.

However, when the film was initially released, it wasn't a financial blockbuster. Only when it was rereleased did it become profitable. Perhaps the movie would have been more successful the first time around if Walt made a change to one of the characters. What if a termite had portrayed Jiminy Cricket?

Nah, probably not, but according to an article in the *Brooklyn Daily Eagle*, from March of 1940, a month after the film's premiere, an ant was briefly under consideration for Jiminy's role.

> When Disney and his staff first plotted out their version of the famed story of the little marionette who comes to life, they didn't even think of having a cricket, or an ant in the picture. Then, one of the boys suggested that it might be good to have some sort of a tiny animal or insect around to bother Pinocchio, whenever the little puppet started getting into mischief.
>
> Because Pinocchio was supposedly made of wood, everybody yelled in chorus that a termite would be the best source of irritation. At this point, a member of the '*Pinocchio*' crew reminded his colleagues that in the original story there was a cricket who warned Pinocchio against trouble in one instance. Pinocchio killed the cricket, but the insect's voice continued with him on his travels, acting, in a way, as a conscience from time to time. Since this cricket appeared in the original story, it was decided to build up a cricket character in the Disney version.
>
> It was Disney's wish that the character be a pompous but good-hearted soul who mixed up his axioms in his tongue-twisting efforts at flowery speech.

When time came to name the new cricket character, everybody around the studio sent in names like Abner, or Marmaduke or Cedric, but Disney said one day: "Why not name him Jiminy? Everybody knows that expression, 'Jiminy Cricket.'" The name, of course, was a natural one.[2]

Here is one last quick story about *Pinocchio*. As we know today, the movie is loved on many levels, from the casual theatergoer to the critics who marveled at the story and animation.

There was one person, however, who didn't like the movie: Paolo Lorenzino, nephew of Carlo Lorenzino. Carlo was the Italian author of *The Adventures of Pinocchio*, written under his pen name, Carlo Collodi.

On January 17, 1941, the *New York Times* published an article stating that Paolo petitioned the Italian Ministry of Popular Culture to sue Walt Disney for libel on the charge of distorting the Italian character of Pinocchio in film and portraying the long-nosed fellow "so he easily could be mistaken for an American."[3] Naturally, nothing significant came from this lawsuit, but it's an interesting side note nonetheless!

April 2, 1940

Mickey Mouse goes public!

If having a Mickey Mouse watch wasn't enough to satisfy your need to own a part of Disney, in April of 1940 the public was officially offered the opportunity to own a piece of the mouse.

Roy and Walt were hoping their little family business would raise $4 million of new capital by offering 150,000 shares of 6 percent convertible preferred stock. Despite their success with Mickey Mouse and *Snow White*, the studio was still borrowing heavily from Bank of America.[4]

As the news of the day states, "the proceeds of financing will be used to pay promissory notes held by Bank of America Trust and Savings Corporation of California. The proceeds of the notes were used for construction of new plant facilities for the company in Burbank, California."[5]

Moreover, there were external factors that were looming over the studio that caused some uneasiness, and the additional capital would provide more stability. One such factor was World War II. The studio earned a substantial amount of money abroad, and with the war raging, there was some uncertainty about the future.

The other factor was Walt himself. Walt was a one-man show. Roy secured the funds and took care of the business aspect, but the creativity and control were all on Walt. Should something happen to him, the studio would certainly be in trouble. When the Disneys filed papers with the SEC to go public, they included this statement: "The company will undertake and insure the life of Mr. Disney for $1,500,000."[4] This insurance policy was going to be a protective feature for owners of the preferred Disney stock. Should Walt pass away on or before April 1, 1944, the policy would kick in, and $1.5 million would be held in a trust to pay the preferred stockholders.

Ever wonder what Walt and Roy earned per year? Well, on the SEC statement of income, the company reported that gross income from *Snow White and the Seven Dwarfs* to December 31, 1939, was $4,577,862.97.[4]

Net income to the enterprise after taxes and expenses was reported as $218,575 for the fiscal year 1935, $78,755 for 1936, $140,627 for 1937, and $918,412 for the nine months ending September 30, 1938. Net income on the same basis for the present company was reported as $1,250,130 for the year ending September 30, 1939, and $64,346 for the three months ending December 31, 1939.

For the year ending September 30, 1939, the executives of the studio received the following salaries: Walt, president, $108,295; Roy, executive vice president, $54,185; Gunther R. Lessing, vice president, $14,335; Edward M. Francis, treasurer, $8,099; and George E. Morris, secretary, $9,711. These figures did not include income from Disney projects abroad.[4]

Just before Disney went public, the brothers both entered a seven-year agreement with their company. Walt received a salary of $2,000 a week, along with certain travel and other expenses. Roy's agreement was for $1,000 a week, along with expenses. It certainly is good to be the boss!

With all of the *i*'s dotted and *t*'s crossed on the financial paper work, on April 2, 1940, 150,000 shares hit Wall Street at $25 a share. An additional 5,000 shares were set aside for employees and officers of the company.[5]

November 13, 1940

Disney's third full-length feature film, *Fantasia*, is released.

Roughly nine months after *Pinocchio* was released, the studio released *Fantasia*, on November 13, 1940. The film is Disney's interpretation of a few classical masterpieces, accompanied by Mickey Mouse. Walt went to great lengths to give the public a different Disney experience. The film features the Philadelphia Symphony Orchestra under the guidance of conductor Leopold Stokowski, along with contributions from Deems Taylor, a music critic and composer.

Fantasia is all about the music and sound effects, and they aren't mere complements to the movie, but, rather, a main focus. The film featured Fantasound, a specialized speaker system Disney and RCA developed to place in theaters showing the movie.

Not to be overshadowed by the sounds of Beethoven, Bach, and Schubert, the studio animators expanded their creativity and explored different methods to capture the classical masterpieces. Here are some details from the *Brooklyn Daily Eagle:*

> Disney and his staff have devised a completely revolutionary medium of screen expression. The animated scenes were not drawn as ordinary Disney scenes have been drawn. Some of them were painted on glass, others on celluloid. Some of them were colored with oils, others in pastels. And all of them—600,000 pieces, and 1,500 backgrounds, many of which move in an opposite direction to that of the animated figure—were photographed by a new 20-plane camera which produces photographic depth and a variety of hues and shades of color, among other complicated things. And, to make the whole thing more revolutionary, the music on the soundtrack was recorded not only before the picture was made but through an eight-channel recording device that picks up an individual section of the orchestra—it's the Philadelphia Orchestra, with Stokowsky handling the baton—when its playing must be highlighted to emphasize the animation on the screen.[6]

August 17, 1941

Walt and members of the studio embark on a goodwill trip to South America.

This entry in the Disney timeline of events has more to it than meets the eye. As World War II raged on, the United States was not yet fully entrenched in battle, yet the situation was intensifying for both North and South America. In the summer of 1941, the US State Department asked Walt Disney to take a trip to South America as part of FDR's Good Neighbor Policy.

Disney's trip would be a goodwill tour of the Latin American countries— showing a bit of Disney and Mickey charisma along with American flair to some countries that may be influenced by or sympathize with Nazi Germany.

On Walt's personal home front, he had a battle waging of his own. It wasn't a war with crimes against humanity, yet it was still a situation that affected him significantly: his animators were on strike and were organizing for a union shop.

The trip couldn't come at a better time, so off they went. Walt and his entourage visited Brazil, Argentina, Chile, and Peru. The trip was successful on many levels. Beyond fulfilling FDR's goodwill goals, the tour provided Walt and his crew the cultural and lifestyle experiences needed to create the Disney spin on the vibrant life of Latin America. Disney films that were direct results of the trip were *Saludos Amigos*, released in 1942, and *The Three Caballeros*, released just two years later. And, as a side note, by the time Walt and his entourage returned home, the studio's animator strike was resolved—Walt's studio was now a union shop.

One member of the crew going to South America was a woman named Mary Blair. Mary joined the Disney studio in 1940 as an artist. She was a integral part of the three-month South American tour. In fact, Mary's work on the goodwill tour was instrumental in the development of *Saludos Amigos* and *The Three Caballeros*.

Mary captured the essence and flavor of the countries she visited via watercolors. Her success documenting the trip with her paintbrush led to her becoming the art supervisor on both *The Three Caballeros* and *Saludos Amigos* films. In addition to her work on several Disney movies, we see Mary's unique style and creativity today in the Disney parks. The It's a Small World attraction and the beautiful mural in the Grand Canyon Concourse at Walt Disney World's Contemporary Hotel highlight Mary's artistic genius.

In October of 1944, Mary was interviewed by the *Brooklyn Daily Eagle* about her role in creating the films that were sparked by the goodwill tour. The interview gives some interesting insight into her experience at the studio.

> Mary Blair, who has been in New York for a vacation, is art director for Walt Disney. That's a real job for a young girl who looks more like a screen star herself than the responsible behind the scenes worker who originates ideas for Disney features and follows them through until they are ready for the screen. She says it's fun.

> The only woman artist in the Disney outfit, it was Miss Blair who helped bring *Saludos Amigos*, with Donald Duck and Jose Carrioca, to the movie theaters last year. She gathered her material during a three-month tour of South America, during which she made notes of the highlights of the South American scene—only her notes were sketches. That's the way she presents all her ideas. She has been working on *The Three Caballeros* for the past two years. This new Technicolor film will present Donald Duck again in Latin backgrounds with Jose Carrioca, the parrot, and a new character, Panchito, a rooster.

> These three caballeros will be teamed with three exotic girls, Carmen Molina, dancer; Dora Luv, singer; and Aurora Miranda, Carmen Miranda's sister, in a Brazilian sequence, with dances and songs. Donald Duck has his first fling at a real romance in this film—he's on the make for all three girls.

> Mary Blair has a nickname around the Disney studios, she admits. Sometimes they call her Marijuana Blair, because of the ideas she dreams up.

> Even Mary Blair stands in awe of a new machine that belongs to Walt Disney Studios—it permits a combination of real people and animated cartoons to act together on screen, and

the first real results of its efforts will be seen in *The Three Cabelleros* which RKO Radio will release soon, probably around the first of the year.[7]

Wow, Marijuana Blair? Huh. The conservative 1940s went right out the window with that nickname! As history revealed, goodwill trip or no goodwill trip, America entered World War II, and again, Walt Disney and his studio were called into duty.

December 8, 1941

Uncle Walt works for Uncle Sam. The United States Army commandeers the Disney Studio.

"Yesterday, December 7, 1941—a date which will live in infamy—the United States of America was suddenly and deliberately attacked by naval and air forces of the Empire of Japan."

These were the words President Franklin D. Roosevelt uttered to the American public and Congress, asking for a declaration of war in reaction to the bombing of Pearl Harbor. Not long after, the United States military was mobilized and became a full participant in World War II.

One such mobilization was at an unlikely locale, the Disney studios. Within days of FDR's speech, word had spread that the United States military had commandeered the studio. Due to its location in Burbank, the military brought in antiaircraft and searchlight batteries to station alongside the variety of military personnel they commissioned to the studio.

Aside from his studio becoming a makeshift military post, Walt made a substantial personal contribution to the effort. The August 11, 1942, edition of the *New York Times* chronicled Walt's contribution of two ornamental iron deer from his front lawn. The donated deer were used for scrap metal. They weighed a ton and contained enough metal for one 75 mm field piece, or ten thousand incendiary bombs.[8]

The story of Walt's contribution was a good public relations piece and timed just a few days prior to the *Bambi* release (more on *Bambi* in a bit). In actuality, though, this contribution paled in comparison to the all-out media blitz the Disney studio put out during the war.

In August of 1942, roughly nine months after the military drafted the Disney Studio into the war, *Life* magazine ran a story titled "Walt Disney Goes to War," which highlighted the studio's contributions.

> In just under a year, 90% of the studio's employees, roughly 550 employees were working in some capacity to support the studios war effort. In total, six branches of the government enlisted the help of Donald the Duck or Pluto for propaganda, or more specifically, some training film. Both the Army and the Navy ordered quite a few Disney training films—at the time of this article, the Navy ordered more than 50 films on every war subject from bombing and gunnery to paratroop training, in under a year.[9]

As for why these films were so successful for the military, the *Life* magazine article sheds some light on the Disney success:

> So many Disney artists are fine teachers because, primarily, they know how to hold your interest.
>
> By their highly perfected animated-cartoon technique, they can show you the inside of something—say, an antitank gun—where no camera could penetrate. They can take the gun apart, piece-by-piece. Step by step, they can show a mechanical process. They can show an aviator what to expect flying through thunderclouds or, in a film on malaria, they can make a germ-bearing mosquito so gruesome that nobody could ever forget it.
>
> On his own, Disney is making 18 cartoon shorts to be released publicly next year. Half of them are related to war. With no sacrifice of humor or variety, these films will crusade for the kind of world where a free popular art, using a man's unlimited imagination, can flourish—where everyone has some chance to laugh and learn.[9]

As the war was coming to an end, another article from *Flying* magazine in March of 1945 gave a more detailed look at Disney's military cartoons and a recap of what the Disney studio had produced for the war effort. It also gave a bit more insight into the great lengths taken by the animators to capture what was needed to produce these war films.

Today, Disney and his helpers, far busier than their dwarfs of *Snow White* fame, are engaged in one of the greatest of wartime education projects. They have produced more than 400,000 feet of educational war films for every branch of the service—enough to make a continuous movie 68 hours in length. Last year the studio produced 150,500 feet, 88 percent for the Navy Bureau of Aeronautics, the Signal Corps, and the Army Air Forces.

During 1943, alone, Disney produced 204,000 feet of film. Most of it—a total of 94 percent—was produced for the government at cost. Yet normal production for one pre-war year was 27,000 feet. Streamlined methods of production made possible this increase.

Disney had already achieved considerable fame in all branches of the services by producing without charge hundreds of comic insignia for everything from bomber and pursuit squadrons to PT boats and coast artillery units.

But Disney actually made his first venture in producing battle films in 1939. That year, he produced a series for the Canadian Government covering the operation of the Boyce anti-tank gun plus a number of war bond trailers.

Then, by Spring of 1942, the Disney studios were swamped by scores of orders from our own services. The Navy got there first with a request for 90,000 feet of film to be delivered in three months. Since then, Disney and his staff have dabbled in, investigated, studied, and worried over virtually every government activity, with accent on the aviation branches.

They have produced films for the Co-coordinator of Inter-American Affairs, covered every conceivable subject from aerology (the practical application by pilots of the science of meteorology) and pursuit combat tactics to maintenance of aircraft by ground crews—everything from health problems in South America to electronics, electricity, and superchargers. Their films have been translated into Portuguese, Spanish,

Russian, Swedish, French and Italian. Chinese versions are to undertaken soon.

Staff members have gone up in blimps to photograph submarines, they've haunted airports and air bases, they've ridden on aircraft carriers, they've gone aloft on simulated bombing missions, and they've flown in the fastest of planes.[10]

These stories about Disney's war effort illustrated that the studio could adapt their style and craft to just about any topic. Disney was proficient in teaching and instructing people what to do via their cartoon medium. With that in mind, the United States government figured the Disney concept should also work with the general public.

In 1942, Disney was hired to make an instructional film for the masses; the subject: pay your taxes! Which Disney character was going to dole out tax advice? Who else but Donald Duck.

Seriously, who wouldn't listen to and trust an often ill-tempered, somewhat unintelligible character during tax time! After all, at times Donald's popularity rivaled or surpassed Mickey's, so, according to the US government, he was the perfect spokesman.

Marketability aside, "he was the head of a family, and he supports his three adopted nephews for whose maintenance he has a legal and moral obligation," according to an article in the *New York Times*.

The tax film was titled *The New Spirit*. It was seen in over twelve thousand theaters and instructed millions of Americans how to pay their taxes properly.[11]

Disney was paid $80,000 for the film—although Congress threw a fit and didn't want to pay the studio, despite the fact that there was an increase in people submitting their taxes that year.[12]

As you can see, the war effort kept the Disney studio busy, but not necessarily profitable. In the studio's 1943 corporate filings, Walt received a salary of $50,500 and another $5,288 in dividends for his holdings.

As mentioned earlier, just a few short years prior, when the company went public, Walt had signed an employment agreement paying him $2,000 a week for the next seven years. The war effort cut his salary in half—yet it was still a remarkable salary, considering the state of the world around him.[13]

Times were tough during the war, even for the studio. It struggled financially during the war, and for a period after, but Walt was able to keep the studio going. More importantly, Disney provided an invaluable wartime service in a time of need. Disney filled a niche many other Hollywood studios weren't able to fill. With that being said, let's jump to the summer of 1942 and pick up with one of Disney's most popular films.

August 13, 1942

The Disney classic *Bambi* is released.

Walt Disney expected nothing short of perfection from himself and his studio. Often, outside-the-box thinking was required to accomplish these lofty goals. The film *Bambi* is an excellent example of Disney going the extra mile to achieve realism and supremacy in his craft.

When word got out that the Disney studio was working on *Bambi*, the Maine Development Commission reached out to the studio and offered to send two live fawns to the studio. The opportunity to study the animals from childhood into adulthood would be a valuable asset to the film. The studio jumped at the commission's offer.[15]

Once the deer came to the studio, the animators were given rooms overlooking the deer pens so they could spend hours each day watching their every movement. Right before their very eyes, the fawns began to lose their baby spots, and little bumps started to sprout on their heads, the precursor of antlers.[15]

By the fall of 1938, the studio was working to develop the story, the backgrounds, and the settings. Disney had three crews working on the picture. Walt was so detailed in what he expected for Bambi's forest that he sent someone to Maine to get thousands of photos to emulate in the movie.[14]

A story from the New England Historical Society gives some insight into Walt's requirements. "Disney dispatched Maurice 'Jake' Day to Maine to make thousands of forest photographs. Often beginning as early as 4 A.M. to get the required effects, Jake met such requests as the following: An oak tree after an ice storm. A beaver dam mounded with snow. Cobwebs on the grass. Spider webs covered with dew. Morning and evening showing shafts of light coming through deep woods. Effect of wind on trees before a thunderstorm." Maurice Day, born in Maine, was an animator at the studio.[14]

That is some serious research and development for one film—one that took the studio nearly five years to complete from the time Walt initially purchased the rights. All in all, the Disney animators created nearly two million drawings for *Bambi*, yet only four hundred thousand made the cut.

In another interesting side note, did you know that Bambi was the fawn that gave birth to a bear? Well, Smokey the Bear, that is! In 1944, Disney lent the image of Bambi to a national campaign to prevent forest fires. Bambi was on loan for only one year, and the cartoon campaign was so successful that it was the catalyst for the creation of the Smokey the Bear cartoon icon.[16]

More recently, in 2011, *Bambi* was added to the National Film Registry of the Library of Congress. In addition, the American Film Institute ranked the flick third on the list of the top-ten animated movies, just behind *Pinocchio* and *Snow White*.

November 12, 1946

Song of the South is released

Have you ever enjoyed a trip down Splash Mountain? It truly is a great ride. Perhaps you had the song "Zip-a-Dee-Doo-Dah" stuck in your head, going round and round like a broken record; it is a catchy tune, after all. Well, if you've experienced either of these things, then that's about as close to the movie *Song of the South* as you're going to get!

Song of the South is a combination live-action/animation full-length feature that was released in November of 1946. Due to its controversial themes and topics, there's a good chance you won't see a seventieth-anniversary edition pop up for purchase in the iTunes store.

Good, bad, or indifferent, the movie is a part of Disney history, and it made headlines at the time—lots and lots of headlines. I've included a vast array of them on the website, some good, some bad, and some…well, you'll have to read them for yourself. If you haven't had the opportunity to see the movie—it does pop up on YouTube from time to time—here's a review from the *Los Angeles Times*:[17]

> The picture (haven't you heard?) is *Song of the South—With Uncle Remus and His Tales of Brer Rabbit*, and in it Walt has managed the smoothest integration yet, both technical and dramatic, of cartoon with live action.

The locale is the old South. Bobby Driscoll is a lonely little boy on his grandmother's plantation till he meets up with Uncle Remus. Bobby takes all his little-boy problems to the old Negro, who has a solution for each: how not to run away from home, what to do when you stick your feet in trouble, and where to find a laughin' place (everybody's got a laughin' place).

Uncle Remus illustrates his tales with Brer Rabbit, Brer Fox and Brer Bear, the delightful and "bodacious critters" created originally by Joel Chandler Harris. They are wondrous tales, enhanced, if anything, in raffish humor and excitement by the Disney pen and brush, and every time another one came on the youngster in front of me sat up with renewed expectancy.

Criticism has been raised in the East by the racially conscious that, in portraying Uncle Remus as the stereotype of the lazy, shiftless (but admittedly lovable) southern Negro, the film performs a disservice. Perhaps it does—but at worse, I think in a negative way. For like his stories, Uncle Remus "never done no harm to nobody." Besides, this is the postbellum South as Harris described it.

James Baskett, from radio is wholly ingratiating in the role. The children are charming and natural, Luana Patten, a darling girl, and Glenn Leedy as well as Bobby Driscoll.

The rich music score is interspersed with spirituals and catchy tunes like "Zip-a-Dee-Doo-Dah," "How Do You Do?" and "Laughing Place." But then the while work marks a welcome swing away from Disney's recent sophisticated "revues." In Uncle Remus' own words, it's "mighty satisfactual."

In March of 1948, James Baskett himself was more than satisfactual. Mr. Baskett won a special Academy Award for his portrayal of Uncle Remus. Unfortunately, in July that same year, James passed away at the young age of forty-four.

For what it's worth, in 2016, IMDb.com (Internet Movie Database) rated *Song of the South* 7.4 out of 10 from nearly 8,000 votes. In comparison, *Pinocchio* was rated 7.5 from nearly 90,000 votes, and *Snow White and the Seven Dwarfs* was rated 7.7 with 130,000 votes.

Well, here we are again, at the end of another Disney decade. The first half of the decade was turbulent for the studio, and it was for the rest of the world as well, as the war left very few people or corporations unscathed.

However, as the 1940s came to a close, it marked a significant milestone to celebrate—a birthday. Mickey Mouse turned twenty years old! In honor of this momentous occasion, the *New York Times* ran a piece on Mickey. In the article, film critic Frank Nugent made an attempt to interview Mickey Mouse, but Walt wasn't biting. Instead, he got a pretty informative interview about both Mickey and his alter ego, Walt, late in 1947.[18]

The interview opens with a few interesting facts about the Disney facilities. The studio had a baseball diamond, Ping-Pong tables, a couple of horseshoe-pitching lanes, and a penthouse sun deck where the male employees acquired an all-over tan.

Walt's office suite had a stainless-steel kitchen, a dressing room, a shower, a piano, a radio-phonograph, couches, and coffee tables. Additionally, the facility was fully air-conditioned—an uncommon luxury at that time. Let's jump right into the interview:

> "I want to interview Mickey," I said, taking the mouse by the horns. Walt looked down his nose at me.
>
> "I dunno," he said. "It's a little irregular. We've kinda frowned on direct interviews. The Mouse's private life isn't especially colorful. He's never been the type that would go in for swimming pools and night clubs; more the simple country boy at heart. Lives on a quiet residential street, has occasional dates with his girlfriend, Minnie, doesn't drink or smoke, likes the movies and band concerts, things like that."
>
> "I'd still like to ask him some questions," I said firmly. Walt's fingers drubbed the desk. His employees recognize it as a danger signal, once removed from his rubbing the side of his nose with a straight index finger. But I wasn't on the payroll so I just waited.

"I've always done The Mouse's talking," Walt said. [He never calls Mickey by his first name; he's always The Mouse just as Donald is always The Duck] "He's a shy little feller, so I've provided the voice. I use a falsetto like this. [And he demonstrated.] His voice changed after I had my tonsils out. It became a little deeper. But no one noticed it. I kind of like it better. Sometimes, I'm sorry I started the voice. It takes a lot of time and I feel silly doing The Mouse in front of the sound crew. But I'm sentimental about him, I guess, and it wouldn't be the same if anyone else did the speaking."

The question-and-answer session that continues centers on Mickey's creation and his first few years in existence through the 1930s. When discussing the original incarnation of Mickey, Walt remarked how he was a bit crude in both animation and some of his antics, such as pulling on animals' tails or using certain animals as instruments—things, Walt noted, the audience wouldn't appreciate from Mickey today.

Then Walt mentioned this interesting blurb about Mickey before moving on to discuss one of the other really popular members of the Disney family:

Somewhere in the late Thirties, Mickey lost his tail; a canny production man had figured that thousands of dollars would be saved by not having to animate that eloquent little appendage. But Mickey didn't seem the same without it and the tail was restored.

The modern Mickey—they now know—wouldn't pull a cat's tail to make music and couldn't be found on a chain gang without there being some innocent explanation of it. Mickey is ringed about with musts and must-nots. In addition to not smoking and not drinking, he doesn't use any language stronger than "shucks."

Donald has no such limitations; he can be diabolic even to the point of looting his nephews' piggy bank. Some of the heretics at Disney's will confide that they have more fun working with the duck than with the mouse for just this reason and hint that the public's current preference for Donald over Mickey (the Gallop Audience Research Institute puts Donald first,

Bugs Bunny second and Mickey third) is a vote for human fallibility.

Walt only smiled wisely when I brought this treasonable report to his office. "Sure," he admitted. "After 120 pictures, it's only natural for them to get a little tired of The Mouse. It's tough to come up with new ideas, to keep him fresh and at the same time in character. The Duck is a lot easier. You can do anything with him. But what they forget is that The Mouse hasn't made a picture since the war. He was in one short released in '42. Five years off the screen and he still rates third! Is there any star in Hollywood with a public that loyal?"

After that banter, the million-dollar question was asked—literally. How much does Mickey make a year? Walt wouldn't divulge Mickey's bank balance; however, Kay Kamen, Disney's licensing agent since 1932, was a bit more accommodating.[18]

Mr. Kamen revealed the Disney brand sold about $100,000,000 worth of goods a year. And while Donald may be number one in the public's heart, Mickey is still number one in its wallet.

And Disney didn't, and still doesn't, let its name be glommed onto any old product. Even in the 1940s, the brand declined marketing offers from alcohol, tobacco, and medicine companies. However, they were happy to endorse books, sweaters, watches, foods, comic strips, records, radios, hot-water bottles, baseballs, paint sets, dolls, and yes, even porringers. For those of you not familiar with this word (like the author), it's a shallow bowl with a handle originating in medieval Europe—thank you, Google!

All of these products meant roughly an additional $500,000 to $800,000 a year in net income for Disney throughout the 1940s.[18] Additional income is something the Disney studio was always in need of, especially with a new decade on the horizon—a new decade that would take the studio to new lands.

CHAPTER THREE

1950S

"I can never stand still. I must explore and experiment. I am never satisfied with my work. I resent the limitations of my own imagination." If there ever was a defining quote for Walt Disney—and, as we know, there are countless quotes from Walt plastered on everything from T-shirts to mugs—this quote epitomizes him, especially during the 1950s.

The revolutionary and impactful contributions Walt made in the middle of this decade, 1954–1956, really changed the world as we know it—not merely in an entertainment sense, but in global, technological, and cultural senses.

In a few short years, Walt built a foundation and began to mold the time we spend with our families. The 1950s brought Uncle Walt into our homes like never before, grooming us to make a trip to his "home." Through his television agenda, Walt was even influential in helping man leave his home planet—not bad for three years' work. But before we get to the apex of the decade—something all of you Disney park junkies have been waiting for, let's start with the girl who lost her glass slipper.

February 15, 1950

Cinderella is released.

On February 15, 1950, Disney's version of the centuries-old folk tale *Cinderella* debuted. The film was a critical success, earning three Academy Award nominations, and it even stands today as a beloved Disney classic.

The *Brooklyn Daily Eagle* gave the film an excellent review a month before its premiere. Let's have a look at some of the highlights.

> Every girl who sees Walt Disney's magical musical, "Cinderella," will see the image of herself and a symbol of her dreams in the title character. And every boy will see in Cinderella, the girl of his dreams. That is the way Walt Disney

planned it during the six years the picture was in preparation and in production. Ever since, in fact, he started thinking about filming this famous love story, which was long before he filmed "Snow White and the Seven Dwarfs."

Cinderella is more than a fictional personage: she is a symbol and synonym. To assure that she would be the personified ideal of million of girls and women, Disney decided that no living star could portray her. The picture had to be entirely cartoon.

As the symbol of all the world's lovelorn maidens, Cinderella is a blonde of medium height, and her weight is about 120 pounds. She has poise, a fine carriage and is universal in spirit and character. She has a pleasant voice, a sunny disposition and a sense of humor. It is all this that wins the heart of Prince Charming.

To complete the Cinderella characterization, Disney interviewed more than 400 applicants before he decided that the voice of blond Ilene Woods, the popular radio and television singer, was the ideal one for Cinderella.

Then he selected red-haired Helene Stanley, talented young dancer, and actress, to be the model for Cinderella. Because the picture is all cartoon, neither Miss Woods or Miss Stanley will be seen on the screen though some of the latter's personality may be detected in Cinderella by her fans.[1]

December 25, 1950

Disney's very first television show hits the airwaves.

By 1950, Walt Disney had conquered the entertainment mediums of his choice. However, during the 1940s, there was something new in the air: television.

The TV is right up there with the automobile in regard to how it has changed modern society and culture. What's not to love? This funky box in your family room—or today, just about anywhere—can keep you occupied for hours.

However, for studio executives, this funky box was considered a dicey medium. The bosses in Hollywood were reluctant to dive right into the technology. Most executives figured its pervasiveness could be devastating to their theater business.

Well, Walt, always the forward thinker and willing to take a risk most others wouldn't, was going to take a chance and dangle his toe into the pool known as television.

As the old saying goes, numbers don't lie, and the number of television sets in use rose from six thousand in 1946 to roughly twelve million by 1951, and by 1955 half of all US homes had one.[3]

This new medium was hard to ignore, and by Christmas of 1950, Walt made his small-screen debut on the Coca-Cola sponsored program *One Hour in Wonderland.*

The show was an hour-long holiday-themed program that aired on NBC at four in the afternoon on Christmas. In attendance were Charlie McCarthy, Mortimer Sneed, Bobby Driscoll, Kathryn Beaumont (the voice of Alice in the upcoming Disney feature *Alice in Wonderland*), and, of course, the man of the hour, Walt Disney.

The show featured a few Disney short cartoons, *Bone Trouble* and *Clock Cleaners*, clips from *Snow White* and *Song of the South*, the tea party from *Alice in Wonderland*, and some of the usual Disney cast of characters adding to the festive party.[2]

The show, of course, was a success. An article from the *Detroit Free Press* a few days after the show's premiere tells you all you need to know about how the public received the special. The title of the article is "Walt Disney Shows TV How It's Done"; clearly it was going to be a glowing review.[4]

> Walt Disney's hour-long Christmas production, "One Hour in Wonderland," the premiere showing of Disney's celebrated characters on television, must have struck despair into the hearts of most of the people who earn a living in the medium. There is nothing in television even remotely comparable to Mickey Mouse, Donald Duck, Dopey, Goofy, Pluto and the rest of them. And there isn't likely to be ever.
>
> Disney is an artist with one eye on the ledger. He once told me that *Snow White* was his own favorite of all his pictures. When I asked why he remarked simply: "Because it made the most money."
>
> This isn't entirely avarice. Disney wants as many people as possible to see his work and that is why he went on television in the first place. "This is not the beginning of a regular

television series for me," he said, "but rather an experimental effort to reach millions of people who might otherwise never see our motion pictures. I've always felt a keen dissatisfaction over the fact that out of 150,000,000 people in America, only about 20,000,000 ever see the greatest of our films."

The kiddies and the adults, too, could hardly ask for more of a Christmas afternoon. Mr. Disney captured 90 percent of the available television audience, which must comprise a good many of those 150,000,000 people he was complaining about.

Despite the fantastic reviews, *One Hour in Wonderland* was only a trial run in television. Unfortunately, it would still be a few more years before Walt would make a regular appearance in the homes across America, and then his appearances would be even more memorable and groundbreaking, a game changer for the entertainment industry.

December 16, 1952

WED Enterprises found by Walt Disney.

On December 16, 1952, Walt Disney founded WED Enterprises, WED standing for Walter Elias Disney. WED Enterprises, now known as Walt Disney Imagineering, are the research and development arm of the Walt Disney Company, aka the folks who create, design, engineer, and build all of those amazing features we see throughout the Disney theme parks.

Shortly after Walt formed WED in late 1952, a public announcement was published in the newspaper over the course of four weeks. The announcement was a legal formality since Walt Disney Incorporated was transacting business under the newly created fictitious name WED Enterprises.[5]

Since this is a pretty cool piece of Disney history, I'll let you read it for yourself.

CERTIFICATE OF BUSINESS UNDER FICTITIOUS NAME

The undersigned, WALT DISNEY INCORPORATED, a California corporation, hereby certifies:

1. That it is transacting, or will transact, business in California under the fictitious name of

WED ENTERPRISES

such business being in part the designing of amusement parks and the designing and manufacture of amusement park equipment and other products of an entertainment, amusement and educational nature.

2. That the principal place of business of said corporation is situated in the County of Los Angeles.

3. That the name in full of said corporation is WALT DISNEY INCORPORATED.

4. That the place of residence and principal place of business of said corporation is 2400 West Alameda Avenue, Burbank, California.

5. That said corporation is the sole owner of said business, and that no other person, firm or corporation has any interest therein.

IN WITNESS WHEREOF said corporation, by its Assistant Secretary thereunto duly authorized, has signed its name and affixed its corporate seal hereto this 30th day of September, 1953.

WALT DISNEY INCORPORATED
By RICHARD M. GOLDWATER.
(Corporate Seal) Assistant Secretary.

STATE OF CALIFORNIA
COUNTY OF LOS ANGELES, ss.

On this 30th day of September, 1953, before me Anita Garrett, a Notary Public in and for said State and County, personally appeared Richard M. Goldwater known to me to be the Assistant Secretary of WALT DISNEY INCORPORATED, the corporation that executed the foregoing Certificate of Business Under Fictitious Name, and known to me to be the person who executed the same on behalf of said corporation, and acknowledged to me that said corporation executed the same.

IN WITNESS WHEREOF, I have hereunto set my hand and affixed my official seal, the day and year in this certificate first above written.

ANITA GARRETT,
(Notarial Notary Public in and for
Seal) said State and County.
(Publish Oct. 8, 15, 22, 29, 1953)

February 5, 1953

The film *Peter Pan* is released.

Scottish author J. M. Barrie's tale of the boy who never grew up started out as a theater production in London in 1904. The following year, in 1905, it came stateside and hit Broadway. By 1911, Barrie released the story as a book titled *Peter and Wendy*.[6]

In 1953, Walt sprinkled some pixie dust on the tale and molded it into the Disney film we know today. Walt wanted to release his version much earlier than the 1950s, but Barrie bequeathed the rights of his story to the Great Ormond Street Hospital in London, and it took Disney quite some time to negotiate the rights to create the film.

In its debut in 1904 in London and then on Broadway, Peter Pan was traditionally played by a woman—this stayed true through the 1950s, 1970s, and 1990s, when Mary Martin, Sandy Duncan, and Cathy Rigby were cast as Peter.[8]

In Disney's rendition of this classic, a real boy, Bobby Driscoll, a child actor whom Walt had cast in several of his features, voiced Peter. Traditionally the stage production utilized a beam of light to represent Tinker Bell. Disney's version allowed Tinker Bell to be seen as an actual character.

As the release date for the film inched closer and closer, the studio went about its usual routine for publicity and interviews regarding the movie.

An article from that treasure trove of Disney news from the 1940s and 1950s, the *Brooklyn Daily Eagle*, featured an extraordinary story a month before Peter Pan's release. What is great about this article is not just the tidbits about Peter Pan, but the information about another character featured in the story, one Mr. Roy Williams. For those of you unfamiliar with Mr. Williams, I will let the article take over:

> Roy Williams draws as easily as he talks. If there's a paper napkin on the table he'll soon be drawing a comic character on it. No doubt, millions of people have looked at Williams' cartoons and laughed—not his paper napkin drawings, but his screen drawings. He is an art director for Walt Disney, in charge of 500 other artists, has drawn many a Disney character himself, and is an authority on Disney's "Peter Pan," which is coming to the Roxy in February.
>
> "'It took 200 men drawing all day for three years to make 'Peter Pan,' said Mr. Williams drawing a Peter Pan himself on

the nearest paper napkin on the luncheon table. "The picture cost $4,000,000, and the audience will see it in an hour and 20 minutes."

Williams looks more like an ex-football blocking guard than artist—or anybody except football guards, for that matter, usually do—has worked with Walt Disney all his adult life, even while he was going to art school, with Disney paying for his training. Six feet in height, weighing 300 pounds, he got his job with Disney 23 years ago. A high school cartoonist at the time, he took a bunch of his drawings around to the Disney studio, then a one-room garage, and asked to see Walt. While waiting, he talked drawing with the office boy. After a half hour or so he began to gather up his drawings.

"Mr. Disney isn't going to show up; I guess," he said. "I'll come back tomorrow."

"I'm Walt Disney," said the "office boy," "and you're hired."

Williams was the 15th man hired. Now the organization has 1,500 employees, and the plant covers 35 acres in Burbank, with the main building that cost $4,000,000.

"Walt Disney has wanted to produce Peter Pan as far back as I can remember," said Williams. "He was talking Peter *Pan* when I first went to work with him. Now, with new techniques and cameras, it has been possible to do the story the way he wanted it done."[7]

Roy Williams, a.k.a. Disney employee number 15, was more than just an employee who helped promote and market the Disney films to the media across the country. During those early days at the studio, he worked on nearly all of the animated shorts; he even designed more than a hundred insignias for the armed forces during Disney's wartime effort.

Aside from being a talented artist, Roy was a jovial character with a playful personality, which he got to display to the country when Walt handpicked him to play Big Roy on TV's *Mickey Mouse Club* for four seasons, which we will visit in a few pages.

Oh yeah, there is one more thing Big Roy is known for. He is credited with designing the legendary Mickey Mouse ears worn by the show's cast and the millions of people who purchase them at a Disney theme park. In 1992, Roy

Williams became a Disney Legend, which is sort of Disney's version of the hall-of-fame.

October 27, 1954

The *Disneyland* television series premieres on the ABC Network.

> Sometimes I wonder why the hell I got into this thing. But we have passed the point of no return, so there's no turning back. Actually, we entered the project without the profit motive in mind. We thought it would be useful to let people know what we are doing here at the studio. And the series will be helpful in developing new characters and interests in which we wouldn't have developed otherwise.

Walt gave this quote to Associated Press reporter Bob Thomas in August of 1954 when Bob asked Walt how he could turn a profit on his newly announced television show, *Disneyland*, which had a budget of nearly $100,000 per episode.[9]

Well, today we know why Walt got involved into this whole television thing. The show was a means to an end, an end that would culminate in one of the grandest projects that would forever change not only the Disney Company but in many ways our society.

Walt's commitment to television and the American Broadcasting Company was an effort to raise and secure some capital to get his real-life Disneyland built. It was a mutually beneficial relationship for both parties. Walt needed money, and ABC, a smaller and still shaky network in comparison to NBC and CBS, both of whom turned Walt down—needed programming.

Thus, a deal was struck: Walt Disney was beamed into homes across America beginning the Wednesday night before Halloween 1954.

When the show debuted on 114 ABC stations, Disneyland was the only hour-long film show on television, and, ever the visionary, Walt shot the show in color despite ABC's claim that color transmission at that time for the network wasn't "economically feasible."[10]

To quote the Bob Thomas article again:

> ABC network unleashes its most ambitious program to date. This is the costly and promising Disneyland, a new venture in TV entertainment.
>
> The new show makes its debut Oct. 27 and will present a different type of program each week. Each will draw from

the wide range of Walt Disney's interests, from space travel to the antics of Mickey Mouse, from American folk heroes to the habits of Alaskan seals.

"We won't make more than 26 hour shows a year," Disney remarked. "The network wants to put on 39 shows a season, so some will be repeated."

Most of the Disney shows will be brand new material. Part of the series will be titled "Man In Flight." There will be three programs on how humans will fly to Mars. The films will show building of the first space station, a shakedown cruise around the moon and the actual landing on Mars.

"Man In Flight" will be among the most expensive Disney shows. Disney has hired noted experts in the field, including Willy Ley, an authority on space travel; Dr. Heinz Haber, space medicine; and Dr. Werhner Von Braun, space engineering.

Disney is also sending a costly film expedition to Tennessee, Kentucky, and the Ohio Valley to make documents on the legends of folk heroes like Davy Crockett, and Mike Fink. The Crockett story begins shooting in Tennessee around Sept 7 with towering Fess Parker as the legendary frontiersman.[9]

As stated, the show fulfilled two needs, one for Disney and the other for ABC, but there was a third motive here. The show gave viewers a sampling of Disney each week in their homes, and for Walt, this allowed him to create a Disneyland infomercial long before infomercials were a thing.

Walt was covertly priming and stimulating each viewer, who was a potential visitor to his park. Through the television series, viewers could watch the park transform in front of their eyes, without ever leaving their homes. They even became familiar with the layout, as Walt produced stories that mimicked the geography of the park with his Frontierland, Land of Tomorrow, True-Life Adventureland, and Fantasyland themes, which paralleled the park.

The viewers loved *Disneyland*, and Walt's return to television was triumphant. The first incarnation of *Disneyland* was a huge success. Here are a few statistics from the first week of January of 1955.

The second report on Disneyland in the national Nielsen rating moves the show from the 10th place to 5th place with a rating of 44.4 and a phenomenal 57.3 share of the audience. In other words, of all the people with television sets on at 6:30 p.m., Wednesdays, over half of them are watching Disneyland.

Based on Disneyland's audience to date, it is estimated that: Disneyland's viewers spend a total of approximately $60,000 for electricity used by their TV sets during each full hour presentation.

Disneyland's weekly audience, if lined up single file beginning at New York City's Paramount Theatre, would stretch 13,524 miles—or 5,603 miles further than the distance from the theater to Calcutta, India.

Disneyland's audience for "Davy Crockett, Indian Fighter" (Dec 15) number more than three times the total population of the United States, at the time Davy Crockett was fighting the Indians (1820—pop. 9,638,000). That doesn't seem too bad of a record for less than three months on the air.[11]

As mentioned, the show's audience for Davy Crockett was quite large—well, maybe large is an understatement; it became an all-out Crockett craze. Davy Crockett on television led to a Davy Crockett repackage for theaters.

Next were the show's music and the recording of "The Ballad of Davy Crockett," which topped the charts and sold millions of albums. There was even a prequel film, *Davy Crockett and the River Pirates*.

One can't forget the thing Disney does best, merchandising. In the case of Davy Crockett, it came in the form of the coonskin hats. In April of 1955, *Life* magazine gave a glimpse of what it was like to be crazy for Crockett.

> The Crockett craze, unexpected even by the watchful Walt Disney, has produced a corresponding frenzy in commercial circles. Dozens of manufacturers are hustling to turn out more than 200 items, from baby shoes to wallets, which might conceivably be connected with Crockett's life. By June, they will sell to the retail tune of $100 million—just about the largest feat of its kind. Meanwhile, Walt Disney has made a full-length movie out of his TV film and booked it into 950 theaters for its opening month of June. Sixteen versions of the Crockett ballad, which was introduced on the TV show, have been recorded, not counting the "Davy Crockett Mambo."[12]

If that paragraph didn't assure you that Davy Crockett was the best thing since sliced bread, the article claims that since the Crockett craze took hold of kids all over the country, the price of raccoon tails skyrocketed from two cents a tail all the way up to eight cents a tail![12]

From raccoon tails to spaceships, we now leave Frontierland and head on over to Tomorrowland, where many believe Disney helped to nudge the government into space exploration.

At the conclusion of World War II, the US government created a program known as Operation Paperclip. Under Paperclip, select German scientists and engineers, some 1500 of them, surrendered to the Allied forces and struck an agreement to move to the United States to continue their scientific work for the US government. Their previous Nazi affiliations would be expunged and forgotten for the greater good of advancing US technology and research.[13]

One participant in this OSS-sponsored program (the OSS was the predecessor to the CIA) was a rocket scientist named Wernher von Braun. Wernher had developed the V-2 rocket, which was the world's first long-range guided ballistic missile—a game changer during the war, as thousands of these had rained down on the Allies.

In late June of 1945, von Braun was transferred to the United States and began his career for the army. By 1952, he was fully entrenched in his career in rocketry and aeronautics and wanted to share his love of space with America.

That year, *Collier's* magazine published a piece crafted by von Braun, "Man Will Conquer Space Soon," which centered on his beliefs about space exploration and a manned space station.

Collier's magazine was great exposure for the scientist to unleash what many believed were just sci-fi dreams from one of the world's best scientists. But if a magazine was good, television could be better, and who better to accompany him, and express his thoughts visually, than Disney.

After the *Colliers* piece, legendary Disney studio animator/director/producer and creative genius Ward Kimball reached out to von Braun to see if he would be interested in working with the studio on a piece for the "Tomorrowland" segment of the *Disneyland* television show.[13]

Wernher jumped at the opportunity and signed on as technical advisor for three of Disney's space-related shows: "Man in Space," "Man and the Moon," and "Mars and Beyond."

Each of these "science factual" episodes was brilliant, witty, and technically accurate, and they captivated the country. However, "Man in Space" was by far the most successful. When the episode aired on March 9, 1955, over forty million people tuned in to watch the episode.[14]

The episode was so successful it was released to movie theaters and even spawned a book. But what could be most impressive of all is the notion that this film may have influenced President Eisenhower to green-light a program for the United States to go to infinity and beyond.

According to the NASA archives, a Marshall Space Center historian documented the von Braun and Disney connection. This is the story about "Man in Space" and the presidential influence.

> In an article published in 1978, David R. Smith, the Disney archivist, reprinted the correspondence between Kimball and von Braun. He also published an account from Kimball which stated that on the morning after "Man in Space" aired, Eisenhower called Disney to compliment him on the show and to request a copy that could be shown to top space-related officials in the Pentagon. Although it is difficult to verify Kimball's account, the story has gained increased attention in recent years. For example, one historian has recently used it to illustrate that, contrary to other viewpoints, Eisenhower was not "hostile to the idea of space exploration or to science in general."[13]

Another take on the story came from a newspaper article from August 12, 1955, titled "Laud Disney for Space Flight Study."

> Since President Eisenhower's approval for launching a man-made satellite to circle the Earth, increased importance and interest is surrounding "Man in Space," the science factual presentation from the "Tomorrowland" realm of the ABC-TV networks *Disneyland.*
>
> The Walt Disney conception of such a satellite—though projected into the distant future—is based on the best current scientific thinking and research by scientists who are likely to contribute to the government project.
>
> For its factual presentation, Disney obtained the services of three ranking space scientists as technical contributors. They are Dr. Wernher von Braun, space engineer, Dr. Heinz Haber,

space medicine authority, and Willy Ley, space travel expert and space historian.

Following the President's announcement, a member of the US Senate praised Disney for his "technical capabilities of great service to our government" in his study of flight into space.

Sen. Carl T. Curtis (Neb) called the attention of his colleagues and of the country to the scientific value of "Man in Space." He entered into the *Congressional Record* an article in which the participating scientists praised "Man in Space" for arousing public support of the space projects.

The article recounted the difficulties faced in obtaining money to finance the race into interstellar space. It described Disney as stepping into the breach, employing space scientists "to bathe the US space horizon with a dazzling prospect."

"Walt Disney," it added, "may be America's secret weapon for the conquest of space. He has discovered the trigger that may blast loose this country's financial resources and place the Stars and Stripes aboard the first space ship as a trial run for an era of interplanetary exploration."[15]

Pretty powerful comments about a program that was rooted in the funding for an amusement park. With Disneyland successfully leaving its lasting imprint on the air, it was time to get Disneyland on the ground. The Disneyland machine kept on rolling, reshaping American society. Next it was time to leave today and enter the world of yesterday, tomorrow, and fantasy.

July 17, 1955

The Disneyland theme park in Anaheim, California, opens for an invited audience.

Well, all of you Disney theme park lovers, the moment is here. We've finally reached the part of the book where the Disney theme parks will command a lot of attention from here on out.

The notion of being able to visit Mickey Mouse at his house in Disneyland or opening up your home to Disneyland via the television in your family room captivated the public and the media's attention in 1954 and 1955. Both projects garnered a lot of interest and were covered meticulously through the press. Let's have a look at how the theme park was described initially by the media.

Here is a sampling of some of the early facts and projections about Disneyland from the news of the day. Some of the initial projections for attendance, the cost of construction and the overall slogans the writers gave to the park are kind of interesting, as they almost didn't know what to expect from this project.

The *New York Times* ran a piece on May 2, 1954, with the title

LAND OF FANTASIA IS RISING ON COAST

Disneyland, Dedicated to the American Ideal and Youth, Will Grow on 160 Acres

Here are a few of the takeaways from the article:

> A cost estimate of $9,000,000 for the building of Disneyland was made today with the announcement that a 160-acre site had been selected for the ambitious amusement center and living museum of Americana by Walt Disney.

> The property, now held in escrow, borders on the town of Anaheim in Orange County. It is about half an hour's drive southeast of downtown Los Angeles over the Santa Ana Freeway. Approximately $1,000,000 is said to be involved in the purchase of the land, which was optioned in fifteen separate parcels. The tract once was part of the historic Rancho San Juan Cajon de Santa Ana. The area is the leading Valencia orange district.

> The project was planned in conjunction with Mr. Disney's entrance into television in association with the American Broadcasting Company, which is owned by United Paramount Theatres, Inc.

> Mr. Disney's contract with A.B.C.-United Paramount Theatres, which is participating in the amusement center operation, is for seven years. The Western Printing and Lithograph

Company of Racine, Wis., which has held exclusive rights to all Disney publications for twenty years, also is associated in the venture. It is also understood that at the end of seven years, full control of Disneyland will be vested in Walt Disney Productions.

Disneyland, which will resemble a giant motion-picture set, is described by Mr. Disney as a "combination" of a world's fair, a playground, a community center, a museum of living facts and a showplace of beauty and magic. Once you walk through its portals, you leave today behind and enter a world of yesterday, tomorrow and Fantasy."[16]

This article was early on in the publicity for the park. It gave a good overview of how the park came to be with the information regarding ABC and the television deal.

As we know today, the construction costs were roughly double what the article estimated. Less than two weeks later, on May 13, 1954, the United Press news agency ran their own story.[17]

Multi-Million Dollar "Disneyland" Will Be Miniature World's Fair

Walt Disney's nine million dollar "Disneyland" project will be a combination miniature world's fair, eighth wonder of the world, and studio for the cartoonist's advent into television.

When the project is completed in 15 months, part of the programs will be filmed there. Meantime, Disney is preparing for the first season's show at his Burbank studio in the biggest deal ever made between a major moviemaker and TV.

Disney figures a person can take in the various rides and exhibits in the park in under 3½ hours, at the average cost of $2. Disney expects some five million tourists and residents to visit the amusement park each year.

Nearly 500 workers at the Disney studio in Burbank are working on the Disneyland project. In a town where gossip is a chief occupation, it is amazing the intricate project was kept quiet. In three rooms draftsmen bend over their boards, drawing detailed plans for the buildings. Nearly everything at the huge park, including a huge paddle board riverboat that will run on a little lake, will be built at the studio.

"The land cost $1,000,000 and getting that was the toughest job," said Disney. "The Stanford Research Institute surveyed the area and selected Anaheim as best. We found one tract out there but when people found out what is was for, the price went up. So we found another section. We had to contact 15 owners, as far away as Ohio, to buy the land."

Around the 56-acre park, next to a 100-acre parking lot, will run an elevated railway that will offer a tour of Disneyland.

You will first enter a replica of a 1910 town, complete with pony-drawn carriages, restaurants, and shops that will sell Disney merchandise. A botanical garden patterned after San Francisco's old Crystal Palace will feature tropical fish and birds.

The next stop in Disneyland will be the "World of Tomorrow." An overhanging monorail car can whiz visitors over the project. Various industries will be invited to put up exhibits of inventions of the future.

Space ship-minded kiddies can step into a rocket ship for a trip to the moon by means of film projected on windows. The seats will jiggle and sound will further the illusion of flight among zooming meteors.

An 80-foot high King Arthur castle will be built in the "Fantasy" section of Disneyland. There will be "Sleeping Beauty" and a museum of Disney characters. One amusement ride will be a flight, a sailing ship over a miniature set of the city of London, as in *Peter Pan*. Or a child can ride into a mine to see Snow White and the Seven Dwarfs or into a rabbit hole to visit a replica of *Alice in Wonderland*.

With a bit more detailed information, this article provides more insight into Walt's dream.

For all you monorail lovers out there, judging from this article, Walt already had the idea bouncing around before the park opened. Unfortunately, the highway in the sky didn't make its Disneyland debut until 1959, when then Vice President Richard Nixon did the dedication.

So what *did* make it into Disneyland, and what was it like on opening day? Well, if you weren't on the guest list for the grand opening, don't worry. Walt was going to bring all of the festivities into your home, live on television.

The ninety-minute live broadcast happened on Sunday, July 17, 1955, from 4:30 to 6:00. ABC broadcasting lined up three sponsors for the show and placed twenty-nine cameras and ten thousand feet of coaxial cable throughout the park—which they claimed was a record amount at the time.[18]

The hosts of the event were Art Linkletter, Robert Cummings, and Ronald Reagan. What these three men provided the guests at home was vastly different from the chaos that ensued from actually being in the park that day.[19]

The Disneyland premiere was like a tale of two perspectives. One was from the comfort of your living room, and the other was from the chaos of actually being in the park. Both perspectives had the same conclusion: Disneyland was remarkable.

The perspective from those in attendance paints a picture of chaos and disorder, but despite the discord, most members of the press still came away in awe of Walt's wonderland.

Here are a few firsthand accounts from some members of the media.

> We made the mistake last Sunday of going to what was called the "press preview" of Disneyland. There were upward of 30,000 people there, with the press in the distinct minority. We understand there was a 90-minute telecast of the proceedings, but we wouldn't know about that. The telecast was designed for the 50,000,000 viewers who couldn't make it in person, and therefore saw a good deal more than we did.

> We saw Davy Crockett and Annie Oakley and 47 children with running noses looking for their lost mothers. Anything else we saw was purely accidental. We don't have x-ray eyes, which is what you need when 30,000 people are standing in one place staring at each other's backsides.

We saw enough, however to get a general idea that Disneyland is the Ninth Wonder of the World, that lives up to all its advance publicity and that a Tuesday morning during the slack season would be an ideal time to go see the place as it should be seen—with some measure of freedom to breathe, walk and see. We never did get within shouting distance of either Fantasyland or Tomorrowland, and about all we saw of Frontierland was an impossibly long line of citizens waiting for a ride on the Mark Twain, the paddle wheel river boat which Irene Dunn christened with a bottle containing water from all the major American rivers.

There is also Adventureland. The line there for the African river boats was even longer than the line for the Mark Twain, everybody apparently figuring to escape the heat by getting out on the water. The successful escapees were few and far between.

To anyone over 30, the most fascinating aspect of Disneyland is Main Street, a faithful reproduction in miniature of an American town at the turn of the century. Every detail is authentic. There is even a nickelodeon featuring the original Mack Sennett comedies, Mabel Normand and the first cartoon ever made.

The discerning eye, of which we have two, slightly bleary at this point, spots one basic feature of Disneyland which most people may overlook—and that is the quality of the place. There is nothing "ersatz" here. Materials used in the buildings are all Grade A, and so is the detail work.

The Disney people are making a point of saying that tourists can go through Disneyland without spending more than $2.00 per person. That is probably true, but it would be like taking a reformed alcoholic on a tour of a brewery. Nothing in itself is expensive, but there is so much to do, so many rides to take, so many really useful and practical souvenirs to buy and so much in-between meal nibbling.

Overlooking the understandable confusion and headaches of the badly crowded press preview and the fact that the park is perhaps 80 percent completed with a good deal of work still remaining to be done, we'd say emphatically that Disneyland is all it's cracked up to be.[20]

This commentary came from Eve Starr, a syndicated columnist on July 25, 1955.

Below is another great article. It leaves the chaos and disorder out of the story and focuses directly on Walt and his park on the big day. There are some excellent direct quotes from Walt, especially toward the end.

The 17 million dollar Disneyland, a combination world's fair and Arabian Nights dedicated to the delight of children, opened today.

A year ago, these 160 acres contained 11,000 orange trees. Today, 22,000 invited guests swarmed through the gates and were dazzled by the wonders of yesterday and tomorrow, concocted by the imagination of Walt Disney and his fellow creators.

"It was nip and tuck, but we made it," sighed Disney. Dressed appropriately for the hot weather, he greeted arrivals in light blue slacks, white shirt with red polka dots and Tahitian straw hat.

"We won't have some of the rides going until the public opening tomorrow," the movie producer remarked. "The Peter Pan flight swayed too much so we can't use it yet. But we'll soon have everything in shape."

Everywhere there were signs of the last minute rush. A painter put final touches on the marquee of the Disneyland Opera House. Workers unloaded crates in the turn of the century stores along Main Street, and a crane hovered over the Mad Hatter's tea party ride.

But most of the fantastic amusement park was finished enough to provide sheer joy for the children of the invited film stars, civic and business officials, and press.

Among the notables ogling the sights: Debbie Reynolds and Eddie Fisher, Irene Dunne, Gale Storm, George (Superman) Reeves, Robert Cummings, George Gobel, and, of course, Fess Parker, who played Tennessee's Davy Crockett in the Disney TV series.

Atop the entrance and circling the entire park are railroad tracks on which travel two steam trains, one is a six car freight train and the other is a miniature replica of a passenger train. Like most of Disneyland, they were reproduced in 5/8 scale giving a wonderland effect to the entire park.

The guests walked into a city square of the 1900 era, bounded by an old time railroad station, city hall and fire station, opera house, and other vintage merchant houses.

Walking further to the city square, the previewers come to the hub of Disneyland, from which extend its four great realms. In one direction was Adventureland, dominated by a large Tahitian hut containing a dining room.

A huge wooden log stockade guards the entrance to Frontierland. Tomorrowland offered the aspects of the World's Fair with its cascading fountains and futuristic buildings. But as Disney himself agrees, the greatest of the realms is Fantasyland. There the Disney creators have lavished their most vivid imaginations.

Disney seemed not at all perturbed by the unfinished portions of the park, "I don't expect the place will ever be finished," he remarked. "That's what I like about it—that it will always be growing."

Walt even shared a funny little story about spending the night working at Disneyland on the eve of the big day. "I finished up last night about 2 o'clock and decided to get some rest, so I got in bed in the little room above the firehouse. Everybody kept waking me up, so I got up and locked the door. When I got up this morning, I couldn't get the darned door unlocked. I had to yell for help."

After a turbulent year of planning and construction behind him, Walt was asked about the need for a vacation. He was asked what he will do next. "Oh, I don't need any vacation," he replied. "I've got things at the studio under control: I think I'll spend my time here for a while." It would appear that the one who enjoys Disneyland the most is Walt himself.[21]

Walt's dream was finally a reality. The preview day provided some highlights and a few lowlights. There were thousands of gate-crashers. Some hopped the fence into the park; others showed up with counterfeit tickets. Mother Nature didn't exactly cooperate either, as it was a sweltering day in July, and, as stated, some parts of the park were unfinished, and the heat only exacerbated the situation. As the preview day for Disneyland came and went, one could only wonder if the public opening would go any smoother the next day. Let's find out!

Honking horns and steaming engines of cars backed up for miles on the Santa Ana Freeway and other roads near west Anaheim Monday morning for the public opening of Disneyland.

The huge amusement area officially opened for business at 10 a.m. Monday after nearly 30,000 guests attended the press preview Sunday. Mind you, most of those guests were uninvited, as Disney invited roughly 11,000 people, the rest gained admission via counterfeit tickets or scaling a fence and hopping into the park.

The public opening drew some 50,000 persons to the $17,000,000 playground and resulted in one of the worst traffic jams in Orange County history.

The traffic began to slowing down at 2 a.m., as early arrivals headed for the huge amusement park eight hours prior to the scheduled opening.

By noon, traffic was so thick on Highway 101 that the California Highway Patrol assigned 30 officers to aid Anaheim city police and Orange County deputies in an effort to keep open the state's major coastal highway.

The unexpected early crowd also forced Disneyland attendants to throw open their parking lots three hours early to get the automobiles off the Santa Ana Freeway in an effort to keep traffic moving. The parking lot was almost filled to its 15,175 car capacity by 10 and hundreds more cars were waiting outside the gates.[22]

Traffic was obviously a nightmare. By 9:00 a.m. 6,000 people were in line. Four and a half hours after the park opened, twenty-four thousand people had gone through the gates. By nightfall, the crowd reached forty-eight thousand—which was eight thousand more than Disney expected for an average twelve-hour day.

Disneyland even experienced its first fire that day, when someone's cigarette ignited a small gas leak near Peter Pan. The fire was quickly put out, and the chaotic park was no worse for the wear.[22]

OK, let us take one last look at Disneyland's debut, this time from a 1950s family perspective rather than that of a member of the press from the preview event. Also, could Disneyland be done for two dollars a person, as Disney stated?

In August of 1955, a husband, wife, and their two children, ages eight and eleven, spent the day at Disneyland. This information came from an article from entitled "Marin Family 'Does' Fantasyland in 10 hours for $29.65, Likes It." Here are a few of their takeaways.

They went midweek and arrived around ten forty-five, forty-five minutes after the park opened. There was already a large crowd on hand, and, as such, the parking lot was getting full, although they didn't need to take the "elephant trains" to reach the entrance.

It cost the family twenty-five cents to park their car. Admission to Disneyland was a dollar for adults fifty cents for children.

> We walked through the gates, into a tunnel under the Santa Fe and Disneyland Railroad tracks and left reality behind. We emerged on the main street of a town of 50 years ago, a town built 5/8th's actual size. It seemed unreal, like a playtown at first. Then because everything was in proportion, our senses

gradually accepted the size and we began to see it as real. It was too real; authentic to the tiniest details.

Disneyland is not shoddy. It is not a carnival or concessions at the beach. It is not false fronts and makeshift rears. It is carefully built by experienced workman. Details are not forgotten, and materials are of the highest obtainable quality.

To match this perfection, the 1000 or more employees at Disneyland are of the finest character. The men and women who operated the rides, sold tickets, or dispensed food were without exception courteous and helpful.

There wasn't a "pitch man" or hawker in the area. The workers were educated and considerate. They alone were a tribute to Walt Disney.

The rides themselves are both unusual and enjoyable. They also are crowded, and in mid-afternoon, it is not unusual for there to be a two and a half hour delay to ride in the tiny cars of Autopia, or an hour and a half in line before Peter Pan.

Some of the rides are as much or more designed for adults than for children. The rocket trip to the moon is impressive; the view from the space station is interesting but fleeting. The ride on the stagecoach or Yellowstone wagon through streams and desert is nostalgic to some who remember the sound of wagon wheels crossing a wooden bridge. The rivers of the world are the most elaborate and most expensive (50 cents adults, 35 cents children) but you'll probably enjoy it even after the wait in line.

Other rides are more strictly for the children, the Mad Hatter's Tea Party, the Dumbo ride, the Casey Jones Jr. train and King Arthur's Carrousel.

What's there to eat? Practically anything you want. We had a late breakfast, so ate only one meal, lunch, there. We ate hot cakes but could have had anything from fried chicken to tacos or hot dogs. There are different restaurants for the type—and price—meal you want.

You can eat a full dinner in the swank Red Wagon Inn from $3.50 down. Or munch chicken at the Plantation Inn for $1.50. Or you can have a 35 cent hamburger and 10 cent cold drink. Or get something from the automat. Buttermilk pancakes were 40 cents and with our drinks and extras, the luncheon bill was $2.16 for the four of us. There are plenty of snacks and cold drinks, even water, available everywhere.

What about the cost of other things? They vary. It costs 10 cents for each such things as a movie—you can stand up to six shows at once. It costs 50 cents for adults and 35 cents for children on the rocket to the moon, but 50 cents and 25 cents on the stagecoach and train. Most of the Fantasyland rides were 35 cents and 25 cents, except those for youngsters, which were less.

Our whole family went on every ride there was, except that we rode the Yellowstone wagon and did not go on either the stagecoach or the burros, which travel approximately the same routes.

In all, the bill for admission, parking, and rides, but excluding food items and trinkets purchased came to $22.05. Food and trinkets, including three sets of gift earrings and seven cents in the penny arcade, costs $7.60, a grand total of $29.65 for 10 wonderful hours.

This may sound like everything costs money. It doesn't. Fully half the time, or perhaps even more, we were inspecting things, seeing exhibits and the wonders of the park which cost nothing. We could have done more. We went on more rides than the children needed or would have been satisfied with. It would have been no trick to cut our expenses by $10. Below that it would have been harder.

Disneyland is an experience. It can well be the high point in the vacation of any family.[23]

Well, there you have it, folks. That last line says it all and applies to each and every one of the Disney parks across the world, even today.

On July 17, 1955, the Disney theme park revolution began. It changed the entertainment industry and the way many of us vacation and spend time with our families, and, for many people, it becomes a lifelong obsession and subculture unto itself.

Any doubts that Walt, his brother, the entertainment industry, or the myriad of individuals involved in this project had were squashed. It may have been a chaotic few days at Disneyland in mid-July, but it was eventually an enormous success, and people came in droves.

By the end of the year in 1957, Disneyland saw its ten millionth guest pass through its gates. As Walt said in the article above, Disneyland would never be finished. The park was alive; it could evolve, grow, and be refurbished.[24]

Before the decade came to a close, additions were already underway at the park.

In December of 1958, an announcement was made outlining the nearly $6 million expansion featuring the Matterhorn, the Monorail, and the Submarine Voyage in 1959.[25]

Here are a few quick stats about Disneyland before we move on. The first-year park attendance was 3,604,351. The second year saw an increase to 4,072,043. Compare that to the combined annual attendance at the time of the Grand Canyon, Yosemite, and Yellowstone Nation Park. Together, these three parks saw annual visits of 3,605,359.[24]

At the time, the Mark Twain held the record for the most-visited attraction, with 3,883,000 passengers, with the Rocket to the Moon blasting off some 2,680,000 riders.[24]

Even in the early days, Disneyland wasn't exclusively a park visited by locals or residents of California. During the park's first three years, 40 percent of its visitors were from outside of the state. The average visitor spent five hours and forty minutes at the park, and roughly $2.79, food not included.[24]

As of 2015, Disneyland welcomed 18,278,000 visitors annually, making it the second-most visited park in the world, just behind the Magic Kingdom at Walt Disney World. And it costs just a wee bit more than $2.79 a person today!

October 3, 1955

The *Mickey Mouse Club* debuts on the ABC Network.

Hot on the heels of the success of both Disneylands, Walt looked to capitalize again with another television program. This time, it would be an hour-long show for children after school, Monday through Friday starting at 5:00, called the *Mickey Mouse Club*.[26]

During the 1930s Mickey Mouse Clubs sprang up across the country at movie theaters. The clubs, complete with officers, would meet Saturday mornings to celebrate all things Mickey—there is a very cool advertisement posted on the book's website announcing the inaugural meeting of the club at a theater in Kansas in August of 1932.

Twenty-five years later, the club still loved their Mickey Mouse, except the venue had shifted from theaters to children's homes across America, and the content wasn't exclusive to Mickey.

The original hour-long show featured newsreels, informative content, live-action programming, a cartoon of the day, and, of course, everyone's favorite, the Mouseketeers.

The episodes even featured content for specific days: Monday could be "Fun with Music Day," Tuesday "Guest Star Day," Wednesday "Anything Can Happen Day," Thursday "Circus Day," and Friday "Talent Roundup Day"[28]

Segments of the shows offered quality educational and cultural programming, and, of course, the show was the catalyst for those infamous Mickey Mouse ears we still see today across the Disney theme parks.

The show was hosted by Jimmie Dodd and featured a slew of children as cast members, most notably Annette Funicello.

Despite being loved by millions across the country, the show in its original one-hour form lasted from 1955 to 1957 and then as a half hour show from 1957 to 1959. The show was syndicated again in half-hour format from 1962 to 1965 and saw a few reboots over the decades.[28]

In 1977, *The New Mickey Mouse Club* premiered but was short-lived. A decade or so later, *The All-New Mickey Mouse Club* had a run from 1989 to 1995 and showcased future stars Justin Timberlake, Christina Aguilera, and Britney Spears.[29]

January 29, 1959

Sleeping Beauty is released.

Here we are in early 1959 with the release of the full-length animated feature *Sleeping Beauty*. Despite Walt's endeavors in television and the colossal undertaking of transforming farmland into Disneyland in a very short period, the Disney studio was still churning out its bread and butter, movies.

In December of 1954, the studio released the live-action film *20,000 Leagues Under the Sea*, which won an Academy Award for special effects and art direction/ set decoration. Then, in June of 1955, *Lady and the Tramp* was released.

Both *20,000 Leagues* and *Lady and the Tramp* were critically and financially successful for the studio. The same couldn't be said for *Sleeping Beauty* when it was released.

The movie took roughly six years and $6 million to produce. The film was released in two formats to theaters—the traditional format and a seventy-millimeter, wide-screen view, a first for a Disney animated feature.

On its initial release, the film brought in only $6.2 million. It wasn't until subsequent releases in 1970, 1979, 1986, and 1995 that the film was considered a success.

An interesting article from the *New York Times* film critic Bosley Crowther in February of 1959 gave a simple explanation to the box-office flop. Pure and simple, the movie was too scary for children. It started out in the vein of *Snow White* and then became too frightening.

> When Mr. Disney tries to make fairy tales for kiddies that will also gratify an adult taste or let's say the taste of teenagers, who are the toughest audience for his films, where must he draw the line on horror, or what his competitors call "hurt," and still get enough melodrama into his cartoons to excite the older kids? Here is the delicate dilemma that has plagued him through the years.
>
> With his "Sleeping Beauty," however, it appears he has given his crew free rein to hit the audience with plenty of violence. For he has a dragon fight in this new fable, at the Criterion, that is just about the noisiest and scariest go-round he has ever put into one of his films.[31]

When the film was rereleased in 1970, one of Disney's "nine old men," Wolfgang Reitherman, who worked on the movie and after Walt's death assumed the role of producer of the studio's animated films, gave some insight into the picture's problems when it was originally released, primarily the wide seventy-millimeter format.

> "Sleeping Beauty" was the first and only animated film made in 70mm (super widescreen) format. When it was first released in 1959, there were few theaters in the country outside of really big cities equipped to handle it. So the audience was limited to begin with.
>
> "Incredible efforts went into its making. The wide screen required more drawing. Entertainment and personalities had to be spread into the side of the screen as well as the center. The film was over six years in the making and cost $6 million. The romance scene alone, six minutes of film cost $ 1million. And that was 1959.
>
> "Disney had in mind a different kind of fairy tale. He wanted more class, more sophistication, more art. I think Walt having made 'Snow White' and 'Cinderella,' wanted a different kind of picture. In my opinion, he had tried to do something different with 'Fantasia' by the use of art, and by doing so, he made it turn out a big cut above the 'cartoon.' In his search for something different for 'Sleeping Beauty,' he hit upon the idea of making use of the 'Sleeping Beauty' ballet music by Tchaikovsky."
>
> Reitherman said, however, that Disney was disappointed that 'Sleeping Beauty' wasn't better received. "He put everything he had into it. And he didn't understand why it didn't succeed. But then he was disappointed when 'Fantasia' and 'Bambi' failed in their first releases. Sometimes vindication comes slowly."[32]

Well, vindication did come for *Fantasia*, *Bambi*, and *Sleeping Beauty*, and you can even throw *Alice in Wonderland* into that mix, as these are all now some of Disney's classic films.

The 1950s were a hell of a decade for both Walt and the studio. If *Sleeping Beauty* was a disappointment for him, all was still OK, as just about everything else he did was prodigious.

As we know, Walt was never one to look back and try to duplicate something he had already conquered. It was about the great big beautiful tomorrow for him. With a new decade upon him, he set out with tremendous and historic plans for the future. Unfortunately, as we all have experienced from time to time, not all of our plans come to fruition, and things have to be put to rest prematurely.

CHAPTER FOUR

1960S

In the late 1930s, Walt invested $2,500 in the Sugar Bowl Resort in Norden, California. In return for his investment, Hemlock Peak was renamed Mount Disney. Some two decades later, Walt had his name attached to a ski resort again, this time as pageantry chairman for the 1960 Winter Olympics at Squaw Valley, California. The games were a success, with Walt redefining the opening and closing ceremonies for future games to come.[1]

As the sports world entered the 1960s with a Disney-influenced Winter Olympics, Walt too was preparing to enter his sixties. By the looks of things, it didn't seem he had any plans of slowing down.

If anything Walt was ramping up again for a great decade. In the summer of 1960, it was announced that ABC had sold back their interest in Disneyland. The *New York Times* reported on the transaction:

> A large stake in Disneyland was sold back by American Broadcasting-Paramount Theatres Inc. last week to Walt Disney Productions and Disneyland Inc. The price for the 35 percent stock interest was a healthy $7,500,000, compared with the $500,000 A.B.C. paid for the stock in 1954. However, over the years, A.B.C. has received no dividends on the investment.
>
> Disneyland, Inc. paid $2,002,500 cash and Walt Disney Productions $5,497,500 in five-year notes. However, the deal also gave A.B.C. a right at the amusement park. It will continue to operate a food concession.[2]

Certainly, Walt was pleased that the outstanding shares were back in the Disney fold, and what better time to assume control than when a major technological innovation was about to debut at Disneyland.

This technological breakthrough was years in the making and years ahead of its time. The debut of Audio-Animatronics—still prominent in *every* Disney theme park—would indeed come to define Disney's creativity and savvy in both research and development and their consistent ability to redefine and amaze the theme-park sector.

June 23, 1963

The Enchanted Tiki Room debuted at Disneyland, introducing the world to Audio-Animatronic figures.

The technology behind the 1960s Audio-Animatronic (AA) figures is rooted in government R&D, specifically a segment of magnetic tape technology utilized on the Polaris Missile, which was a two-stage rocket developed during the Cold War.

The ability to give synchronized sound and movement to inanimate creatures and objects was something Walt had toyed with for over a decade unsuccessfully—the animals in the Jungle Cruise at Disneyland weren't pure AAs in the sense that they were cam driven utilizing hydraulics and pneumatics, and they weren't nearly as advanced. Eventually, he was able to purchase technology from the government and adapt it to his needs.[3]

> It's an offshoot of our work in animation. We started by making the animals move at Disneyland using cams, which can repeat a pattern. Then a whole new area opened up with the release of electronic equipment by the government. Now we can put a whole routine on tape; sound, lip movements, body motions, everything.
>
> The patented process has various degrees of sophistication. They range from one or two simple movements to many complex body actions and facial expressions. Walt's "imagineers" record audible and inaudible sound pulses, music, and dialog on separate magnetic tapes. These are then combined on a single one-inch magnetic tape, which has up to 32 channels or tracks controlling as many as 438 separate actions.
>
> The playback simultaneously relays music and voices to speakers, while sound impulses activate pneumatic and

hydraulic valves within the performing figure. Air and fluid tubes and devices expand and contract accordingly to bring about animation. Sound impulses also control stage and theater lighting, permitting an entire show to be controlled from one tape.[4]

In very general terms, to get from point A to point B, if the Audio-Animatronic was to be of a person, there would be a "model" who was a living person wearing a control harness. The harness recorded all of the actions and gestures the person performed. The movements were recorded on the tape as mentioned above, which were replicated by the Audio-Animatronic.

"All we have to do is set the time, and we can put on shows without even a coffee break." He said the new process had a cost about $1,000,000 in experimental work, would not replace human performers.[3]

This new technology was (and still is) the focus of the Enchanted Tiki Room, where hundreds of birds, flowers, and other critters sing, dance, and talk in a Polynesian setting.

The Audio-Animatronics were—and still are, decades later, albeit the technology has advanced quite a bit—certainly unique and ingenuous in the shows at the Enchanted Tiki Room.

Walt even teased the appearance of more AAs to the press covering the debut of the Tiki Room by telling them the technology would be an integral feature of the "pirate area" at New Orleans Square and the Haunted Mansion, which were under development.

Exciting stuff, but nothing truly captivated the country like the presence of AAs at the World's Fair in New York during 1964 and 1965.

April 22, 1964

Walt Disney debuts four shows at the 1964–1965 World's Fair in New York.

In April of 1964, The World's Fair came to New York, and Disney was well represented at quite a few attractions. Much like the way Walt introduced his viewing public to his creations at Disneyland on his *Disneyland* television program, the same was true for his creations at the fair.

This time, his program was called *The Wonderful World of Color*, and the episode, titled, originally enough, "Disneyland Goes to the World's Fair," previewed the Disney pavilions in early May of 1964.

The program was chock full of Audio-Animatronics, with a behind-the-scenes look at Walt's imagineers creating this new form of Disney magic, which was featured at the Ford Pavilion, the General Electric Pavilion, the Illinois State Pavilion, and the UNICEF/Pepsi Pavilion.[5]

First up is the Ford Pavilion. The motor city behemoth selected the best storyteller in the business to tell the Ford story of yesterday and today.

The focal point of the pavilion was the Magic Skyway ride. Ford dubbed the attraction "an exciting ride in a Company built convertible through a fantasy of the past and future in 12 minutes."[6]

Translation: guests to the pavilion hopped into an actual Ford convertible and were able to enjoy the sights and sounds of the Audio-Animatronic-filled trip.

The cars glided through a transparent glass tunnel, where they were able to see outdoors above and beside them before going back in time via a time tunnel—think EPCOT's Spaceship Earth with lights streaming past you before you make it to the top of the sphere.

Once through the time tunnel, the cars moved through different sights and sounds—AA dinosaurs, cavemen utilizing fire, cave painting, tools, and, of course, tinkering with the wheel.

Next up was a second time tunnel, where guests went thousands of years into the future and visited a city. Guests then exited their four-wheeled adventure and were free to view the rest of Ford's corporate exhibits, which featured their current automobiles along with a few futuristic vehicles.

The Ford Pavilion was a huge hit at the fair. During its twelve-month stint, it hosted fifteen million visitors. Also, some of the technology developed for the track the cars utilized was refined and eventually found its way into the WEDway People Mover at the Disney parks.

The next corporation to feature Disney was General Electric, in their Progressland Pavilion. The pavilion featured the Disney-created Carousel of Progress—it's often said that this attraction was one of Walt's favorites.

The show features a typical American family, (albeit Audio-Animatronic) and shows how electricity, specifically with GE's help, has improved and shaped the twentieth century.

The show's stage is circular and allows the audience to revolve from scene to scene to progress through the century. This attraction was of the most popular ones at the fair, with nearly sixteen million people enjoying it.

A funny story from June of 1965 recounts how a newspaper reporter duped the audience at the show when she hopped up on stage and sat in on one of the scenes and pretended to be an Audio-Animatronic character. She was quite successful!

The article is titled "She Was a Dummy for Walt Disney." With Disney's permission, Joan Crosby hopped into one of the scenes and sat on a couch next to the AA playing the mother in the show and petted an AA cat.

> "I have seen the show four times," a woman said, "and I figured they added a new mannequin. I liked the slippers she was wearing so much I was going to ask the pavilion where they got them."
>
> "What would you say," a gentleman in on the game asked another member of the audience, "if I told you one those figures was real?"
>
> "I know," a woman answered, "It was the dog." The photographer, who was assigned to take the pictures, had not seen the show before. He thought we were all real. After hearing I wasn't, he added: "But that was your cat, right?"
>
> But the best comment went like this: "I knew that figure on the right of (me) wasn't real because her bra didn't fit right."
>
> As the theater revolved to the next stage, the audience was informed by one of the hostesses that one of the figures has indeed been real. They were surprised, which only goes to prove that if you tell people they are about to see Walt Disney's amazingly lifelike audio-animatronic figures talk and move, that's what they will figure they are seeing.[7]

Well, there you have it: nothing gives away an Audio-Animatronic like an ill-fitting bra! After the success of the show at the fair, the Carousel was relocated to Disneyland until September of 1973. Then the show was taken on the road, across the country to Walt Disney World in Florida, where it made its debut in January 1975 and has been going strong ever since.

Up next, the Land of Lincoln and the Illinois State Pavilion. The attraction at this pavilion was a subject near and dear to Walt's heart. Ever since Walt was a youngster, he had had a great fondness for President Abraham Lincoln.

Walt showed his admiration for the sixteenth president in a way only he could—by trying to capture the spirit of Lincoln and bring him back to life via an Audio-Animatronic at the fair. But before we get there, we must backtrack a bit.

In mid-May of 1962, Walt gave an interview about a patriotic show he was creating. The show was going to be called *One Nation Under God* and would feature films and "animated figures" to dramatize the US Constitution. The show would touch on the crises that tested the Constitution, primarily the Civil War.

Also, there would be life-size representations of what were then thirty-four presidents. The climax of the show was to be a speech by President Lincoln. At the time of the interview, the show was still very rough, in every aspect from story line to locale. Walt hoped to build a 1,200-seat theater with a 180-degree screen to heighten the impression of audience participation.

If Walt could secure sponsorship from a corporation at Disneyland, the public would be admitted without charge, as this would attract the largest possible audience.

As Walt remarked, "This is an American story that should be told and retold. It must be constantly put before the public. If we ever forget it or take it for granted, it will be too bad for us. But it's not enough to tell people 'This is good for you', you have got to make this sort of show entertaining."[8]

Well, the story would be told, as Walt suggested, just not in the form or exactly how he thought it would be in 1962. At the time, Robert Moses, a powerful city planner from New York City, was in charge of the upcoming World's Fair and wanted *One Nation Under God* for the Fair.

In 1964, Mr. Moses got his wish, and, to some extent, so did Walt. Instead of the pomp and circumstance of Lincoln and all of the presidents, the Illinois State Pavilion featured President Lincoln exclusively, in what was a remarkable performance by Honest Abe.

The state of Illinois paid Disney $100,000, and the fair contributed $250,000 to create the show *Great Moments with Mr. Lincoln*. Disney used his AA technology, along with a copy of a life mask from Lincoln in 1860, to sculpt an exact version of the president's face.[9]

Two months into the fair's opening, "Mr. Lincoln was speaking to an average of 250 people per show, five shows an hour, 12 hours a day and seven days a week for well over 100,000 visitors a month." This despite the fact that, as one reporter remarked, "the Illinois pavilion is located at Gate 2, in a so-called dead area of the Fair"[10]

Much like the response to the Carousel of Progress, people were convinced that Abe was portrayed by an actor. Virginia Marmaducke, director of special events for the pavilion, remarked, "That last season visitors would seek out my office daily and ask 'Now tell the truth. Wasn't that an actor?'"[11]

Needless to say, Lincoln was a great success at the fair, but his stage performance didn't end at the fair's conclusion. Once his run was over in New York, he was relocated to Disneyland in the summer of 1965, and has been educating millions of folks ever since in various incarnations of the show over the decades.[16]

As for the original aspect of the show that would feature not only Abe but also his fellow presidents, we would have to wait until 1971, when this concept debuted in Liberty Square at Walt Disney World with the Hall of Presidents.

Last but not least, we have the Pepsi-Cola/UNICEF pavilion and the It's a Small World attraction. Now, even the most casual Disney fan is familiar with the attraction itself, so let's just give a brief rundown of how it came to be.

Here's a blurb from the actual 1964 Pepsi-Cola World's Fair brochure.

> UNICEF stands for the "United Nations Children's Fund" and Pepsi-Cola takes pride in saluting this great international organization. Within the Company's two-acre fair area, the United States Committee for UNICEF operates its own

pavilion and exhibit, furnished by Pepsi-Cola, to dramatize UNICEF's role in helping meet the needs of children in over 100 developing countries.

A highlight of the New York World's Fair, "It's a Small World"—a salute to UNICEF, was conceived and created by Walt Disney to honor the United Nations Children's Fund. This attraction was made possible through the generosity of the Pepsi Cola Company.

At the foot of the Tower of the Four Winds, one of the Fair's tallest structures, the UNICEF pavilion and garden are ready to welcome you. Books, games, records, posters, maps, free literature will tell you more about "all the world's children."[12]

So Pepsi was collaborating with UNICEF on a pavilion for the Fair. In turn, Pepsi reached out to Disney to create their attraction. Disney put a concept together for the pavilion, and, with a bit of Hollywood influence—from someone other than Walt—the Pepsi/UNICEF/Disney deal got done.

It appears Pepsi was vacillating and dragging their feet, so to speak on their pavilion. So Joan Crawford, who at the time sat on the Pepsi's Board of Directors (her late husband, Alfred Steele, was CEO before he passed away) made sure the pavilion featuring a Disney concept came to be. So you have "Mommie Dearest" to thank for the "Happiest Cruise That Ever Sailed" and the repetitive, yet iconic theme song, we all know and love![13]

The UNICEF pavilion, like the other Disney-crafted pavilions, was a great success. Nearly 47 million people paid to see a Disney production during the twelve-month stint at the fair.[14] Keep in mind the total attendance of the fair was 51.6 million people, so more than 90 percent of fairgoers saw a Disney production—quite impressive.[15]

Disney's participation and success in the fair were multifaceted. To Walt, the overwhelming success of his projects on the East Coast only solidified his speculation that Disney could thrive back east and that one of his projects would be successful on this side of the country.

On a smaller yet still significant level, Disney was able to tweak and perfect his Audio-Animatronics, which operated in each and every one of his projects at the fair. Eventually, attractions such as It's A Small World and components of much of, if not all of, the other attractions there found their way into a Disney theme park in subsequent years.

August 29, 1964

Mary Poppins premieres at Grauman's Chinese Theatre. The iconic film goes on to win five Academy Awards and the hearts of young and old alike for generations.

Supercalifragilisticexpialidocious! We're at the part of the book that isn't quite atrocious! Yes, here we are in 1964, with everyone's favorite nanny, Mary Poppins. Everything about this movie has reached iconic status in our culture.

At the Thirty-Seventh Annual Academy Awards, the film was nominated a whopping thirteen times, with several aspects of the film, from the acting to the music to the editing, scoring the coveted Oscar. The film was, and still is, a blockbuster. Even today, the film resonates with young and old alike.

But perhaps the film resonated most with the brilliant man behind the picture. Interviews over the years describe Walt's affinity for the movie, particularly the music. The Sherman brothers, the brilliant and gifted song duo, recounted on numerous occasions Walt's love for the song "Feed the Birds."

There was another aspect of the movie Walt loved: the profits! Roughly a year after the release of the film, Walt spoke of *Mary Poppins*'s success.

> Walt Disney picked up the telephone and asked the studio executive: "What's the latest projected gross on 'Mary Poppins'?"
>
> Disney listened for a moment, a faint smile on his face. "Forty million, huh?" he said. "Well, we're getting right up there where Sam Goldwyn said we'd be." The movie maker put down the phone and explained: "After Sam saw 'Poppins,' he called me up to say how much he enjoyed it and how it was the kind of picture the industry should be making. He said he was going to take ads saying so. I told him he needn't, but he went ahead with full-page ads in all the trade journals. He also told me the picture would bring in $50 million in rentals. I thought he was exaggerating at the time. Now I don't think so."[17]

As Walt remarked above, the film was a juggernaut financially. Obviously at this point, the studio was financially stable and profitable, but *Poppins* took them to the next level and allowed for additional growth. Remember back in the 1950s, Walt created a division called WED; it created the attractions for Disneyland. Well, flush with cash from *Poppins*, Walt created another division that manufactured some of the creations WED dreamed up. The name of this division was MAPO, named for its "benefactor," Mary Poppins.

However, for Walt, success wasn't always an easy thing to wrangle as the head of a Hollywood studio. After *Poppins* he had to keep himself and his studio grounded and not get caught up in the whirlwind success of the film. Here are a few more thoughts from him regarding the movie's success:

> But such a triumph also has its drawbacks; Walt sighed as he commented: "Now, whenever we discuss new projects, the people here say, 'It'll be another Poppins.' I have to keep telling them, 'Don't say that. Each picture has to be different.

> "The same thing happened to me with 'Snow White.' It was a big success, and people kept expecting more of the same. We brought out 'Pinocchio,' and it flopped. Then came 'Bambi,' and it did nothing. The war came along and took away our foreign market, and we were in trouble. It wasn't until after the war when 'Pinocchio' and 'Bambi' were re-released that we began to get our money back from them"

Walt was then asked if he would try to cash in again and do a sequel. The answer, of course, was a resounding no.

> "People also said we should do another picture with the dwarfs. They were good characters to work with, but I said that the picture would be its own sequel. You could bring it back every few years for the new generations. We've done that, and it has worked out fine.

> "Plus, Julie is priced out of my range," Walt grinned. She reportedly played Poppins for $150,000; latest price quoted: $750,000 plus 10 percent of the gross."[18]

As history illustrates, everyone associated with the film reaped its rewards, either financially, professionally, or both. So how did it all come together? Since

Disney did an excellent job on the backstory of Walt, P. L. Travers, and the Sherman brothers with *Saving Mr. Banks*, let's have a look at how Julie Andrews and Dick Van Dyke came to create such magic on the screen.

"Not photogenic." "Not sexy enough to be a movie star." Did you ever think these words could be used about our beloved Mary Poppins, aka, Julie Andrews? Well, apparently, this was the knock on Julie Andrews in Hollywood, and Julie knew it.

> "I suppose the movie people didn't consider me photogenic," she remarked while doing press for *Mary Poppins*. Poppins was Julie's first film role, as she was known primarily for her stage work on Broadway, most notably in *My Fair Lady*, where she starred as Eliza Doolittle in the Broadway premiere of the production.[19]

Despite rave reviews on Broadway, Julie was passed up for the role of Eliza—a role she created—when Warner Brothers made the story into a movie. Instead of Julie, Audrey Hepburn got the nod. Despite the snub, Julie took the disappointment in stride.

> "I had steeled myself against it," she explained. "I knew that they wanted a movie name, and I had never been in a film. I reasoned that with most musicals—'South Pacific,' 'Gypsy,' etc.—they don't use Broadway stars for the movie.
>
> "Still I did get a slight 'boing!' when the news came. I must say. I would have been more upset if it had been anyone else. She should be marvelous in the part." "She," being Audrey Hepburn.[20]

In hindsight, it was a great thing for Julie that she didn't get the part, as Walt was preparing to film *Mary Poppins* at roughly the same time.

One afternoon, Walt saw Julie in a production of *Camelot* and asked to see her in her dressing room after the show. He spoke with her about his upcoming film project. Here is a bit more from Walt:

> "The boys and I went to see Julie in Camelot in New York. We knew her voice was exactly right from her records, but there was absolutely nothing of her on show in the way of

a screen test. However, we were all captivated by her stage performance—the hint of comedy lurking under the romantic charm—and we were even more captivated by her personality backstage in her dressing room.

"Julie with her agent and manager came out to California to listen to the songs and see exactly how we meant to adapt the book. But still Julie held back from signing. Secretly I reckon she was still hankering for her old part in 'My Fair Lady' on the screen.

"Then one evening when Julie and I were having a drink together, her manager arrived with the evening paper, and there it was at last in black and white. Audrey Hepburn was to play Eliza on the screen.

"Julie lifted her glass and said: 'Let's drink to Audrey's success. If I couldn't have the part, there is no one whom I would rather have it.' After which I said: 'Now let's drink to Mary Poppins,' and we clinked glasses together. The next morning she signed."[18]

Julie went on to remark about Walt and the film, "He wooed me, and won me. He had a fine script."[21]

And, as the saying goes, the rest is history! Julie reigned triumphant not only against the naysayers who claimed she wasn't a good fit for the big screen but also against the film *My Fair Lady*.

Both *Poppins* and *Lady* were released the same year, and while Hepburn and *My Fair Lady*, were critical and commercial successes, they weren't to the magnitude of *Poppins*.

My Fair Lady received twelve Academy Award nominations to *Poppins*'s thirteen. Julie Andrews received the Academy Award for Best Actress, whereas Audrey Hepburn wasn't even nominated for her role.[22]

Now let's have a look at Dick Van Dyke's role as Bert. Van Dyke's casting as Bert wasn't as dramatic as Julie Andrews. Dick was already a star on stage, screen, and television, but if you ask him, he thought his career would be short-lived. Perhaps some critical comments he made about the film industry sparked one producer's interest in him.

Van Dyke once described his movie and television successes as a "quirk of fate." On another occasion, he said, "Probably three years from now, I won't be able to get arrested."[23]

Dick believes Hollywood's film fare has consisted of too many downbeat movies, which were shunned by the family trade. Van Dyke practices what he preaches. He once preached from the pulpit of a Hollywood church, where he criticized movie producers whose films border on obscenity. "I've turned down some movies because I didn't think they were right," Dick said.

"They were leading man roles in light comedy, and all so much the same. They all had the bedroom scene."[24]

Academy Award–winning producer Disney is quoted as saying that he heard Van Dyke's remarks about Disney Studios making good movies, films that families could watch. "I decided to have a look at the young man," said Disney, who met Van Dyke and signed him to a costarring role with Julie Andrews in *Mary Poppins*.

"I should have done this picture 20 years ago," said the 37-year-old Van Dyke. "I only started dancing three years ago, and I'm already too old for it. And in this picture, which has some animated characters in a fantasy scene, I'm dancing with partners who aren't even there. The animated characters will be painted in after they shoot the scene."[24]

Van Dyke is not an actor who wants to star in problem pictures. His opinion of the "Poppins" film is based more on personal conviction than the usual actor's ego.

"This is going to be the greatest family picture of all time," he said. People in films always feel this way about their latest picture, but years from now, movie fans will have forgotten "Cleopatra," but they'll still be seeing this picture.[24]

Well, there you have it. You heard it from Bert himself! The movie is certainly right up there as one of the all-time greats for the family. The movie (and music) is firmly imprinted in our society as a rite of passage during one's childhood.

Today, Walt would be proud not only of its legacy and impact over the decades but on the studio's roughly $6 million investment that today has yielded a lifetime domestic box office gross north of $100 million.[25]

July 17, 1965

Disneyland celebrates its tenth anniversary.

July of 1965 marked ten years for Disneyland. Before the park opened, many in Hollywood and the media dubbed it Disney's Folly, as the consensus was the park was going to be an epic failure.

Walt wagered everything he had and a substantial amount that he didn't have to see his world-changing dream come true. The park was not only one of his dreams realized, but it became part of the dreams of millions of people across the world as over fifty-two million passed through its gates (at this time).

Aside from the millions of visitors during its first decade (as high as sixty thousand people in a single day), the park had a few other notable moments. In 1962, the park was the setting for a movie, as *40 Pounds of Trouble*, starring Tony Curtis, was filmed on location. The movie was a first, as all previous requests (upward of twenty) to use Disneyland as a backdrop in a feature film had been denied by Walt.[26]

For all you foodies out there, the park was even the locale for the creation one of the country's favorite snack foods, as Doritos were born at Disneyland's Mexican restaurant, Casa de Fritos.[27]

Over the course of a decade, Disneyland welcomed eleven kings and queens; twenty-three presidents, heads of state, or prime ministers; and twenty-five princes and princesses.[28]

But you didn't have to be a world leader to visit the park; all were welcome at Disneyland. Well, all but one. In 1959, the leader of the Soviet Union, Nikita Khrushchev, wanted to drop in and see Mickey Mouse but was denied entry.[28] And in typical Khrushchev fashion, he threw a fit. I guess Mickey Mouse made capitalism seem OK for that day!

As Walt often commented, the park would never be complete, as changes and growth were always afoot. In 1965, the park grossed about $27 million, and Walt was continually trying to build a better mouse and reinvest profits back into his kingdom.[28]

An additional $35 million or so had already been added to the park since it opened, and there was more on the horizon. Around the time of the tenth anniversary, Walt added another star to his crown, an improved and more realistic Audio-Animatronic Abe Lincoln capable of 275,000 separate motions, a vast improvement over the Honest Abe that wowed at the World's Fair.[29]

Additionally, Walt and his team were steadfastly working on the first new permanent addition to the park in the way of a "land," New Orleans Square. Based on the New Orleans of yesterday, this area opened in July of 1966 and would feature two new attractions Walt was overseeing, a pirate attraction and a haunted house of some sort. Neither attraction was complete when New Orleans Square debuted in 1966.[30]

With the creation of an entirely new land at Disneyland for the first time, was Walt getting the itch to create again? Perhaps something bigger and better than Disneyland? Was this even imaginable after just ten short years? Well, there were some rumblings all the way across the country in a different Orange County, this time in Florida.

November 15, 1965

Walt and Roy announce their plans for the "Florida Project."

Years of success at Disneyland had people from far and wide urging Walt to bring his park (or some form of it) to their neck of the woods. Always a reluctant participant in sequels, the answer was usually a resounding no. As Roy Disney often said, "Walt instinctively resists doing the same thing twice. He likes to try something fresh."[31]

But briefly for a period in 1963–1964, there was a glimmer of hope for the folks living in Saint Louis. There was going to be a Disney park in the Midwest. As the *New York Times* covered it in July of 1964,

> The new Disneyland, which is scheduled to be built in St. Louis, will bear little similarity to its predecessor. While Disneyland sprawls over 67 acres, the St. Louis amusement center would probably cover about 2.5 acres and rise as high as five stories. Construction is not expected to be completed until 1966 or 1967.

Disney officials are wary about discussing the St. Louis project because final details have not been worked out. The new Disneyland would be part of a massive 465-acre urban renewal project aimed at remaking the entire waterfront area of St. Louis."[31]

Whoa, not so fast Mickey! Don't pack your bags for the Show-Me State just yet. Walt Disney's Riverfront Square sounded great on paper, but that's about as far as it got.

In March of 1963, Walt met with the mayor of Saint Louis, Raymond Tucker. The two discussed the plans for an enclosed five-story park sprawled over two blocks in the heart of town. Blueprints were even drawn to conceptualize the project—the complete thirteen-page set was sold at auction in late 2015 for $27,000.[32]

Unfortunately for the city of Saint Louis, a disagreement over funding eventually derailed the project, and Walt moved on. It wasn't long, however, before another state would land Disney and set the world spinning with news of a bold new Disney project.

Now, before we read about the brothers Disney's venture into Florida, a bit of a disclaimer. There is an old saying—there are three sides to every story: your side, my side, and the truth. In a sense, this is somewhat applicable to the Florida Project. There was the project when Walt was alive; the period after Walt's death, when the project was in limbo; and then, ultimately, what came to fruition, Walt Disney World as we know it today. We will see each of these sides over the next several pages, with Walt's death acting as the line of demarcation.

Now, with that being said, the next few pages that end this chapter and open the next will try to cover an expansive and transitional period for the company. Each segment is not in extreme detail, as entire books have been written on this period of Disney history. However, what is offered is a general scope, with tidbits from each of these "sides," hopefully providing you with a unique perspective of the project as a whole and of how the Florida Project evolved and came to be Walt Disney World. Now back to it!

Roughly a year or so after Disney flirted with Saint Louis, they landed in Florida, although their land purchase was still a bit of a mystery in the dawn of the story.

The local newspapers were tracking secret land deals in Central Florida. A plethora of speculation and mystery about which company was purchasing large tracts of land in the area started to garner a lot of interest. One name that continued to pop up in the conversation was Disney. The company adamantly denied their involvement in the land purchases. Walt himself even sidestepped the question himself in an interview published on October 19, 1965.

> "There will only be one Disneyland—as such," he replied with a smile, and one could read a lot into those last words. "I've heard those rumors and reports from Florida," Walt said. But then did not take them out of the rumor category. "I have studied Florida. I visited all the big attractions. I wanted to see how they did things and how they handled the crowds. You have some beautiful spots in Florida. I've seen them. But you some problems."[33]

Well, about a week later, the cat—or, shall we say, the mouse—was out of the bag. On October 26, 1965, Florida Governor Haydon Burns was speaking at a state meeting of municipalities in Miami and remarked that thirty thousand acres purchased near Orlando was indeed Disney, and they were ready to begin construction on an eastern division of Disneyland.[34]

When reporters reached out to Disney, they pushed back on the story and said they had no construction plans, and "it should be emphasized that the Disney firm is considering possible locations in other parts of the nation for a project such as the one described by the Governor in his Miami talk."[34]

The very next day, the governor confirmed again that it was indeed Disney coming to Central Florida, and he was meeting with the company within the next two weeks.

Disney was on their way to Florida, and, as one reporter commented at the time, Walt would be the most celebrated visitor since Ponce De Leon, as the project wouldn't be a two-block entertainment center or a sixty-five-acre theme park like Disneyland, but an enormous project.[35]

The land alone was over forty square miles. The country and the locals especially were eager to hear about the plans for the property. Even with the excitement of the new enterprise, there were already a few rumblings by locals about how much the state would have to concede financially or municipally to keep Disney happy.

On October 27, 1965, Governor Burns said the deal would be routine:

> On November 15, he said a meeting of state, county and municipal officials and Disney representatives will outline areas of "cooperation," which the state will have to guarantee to get the attraction built. 'They are not asking for any handouts or any concessions which any other industry would not receive,' he said. He pointed out that one of the areas of cooperation will be the creation of two new cities, which will require the action of the 1967 session of the Legislature."[36]

Surely the "creation of two new cities" is business as usual for welcoming a new enterprise into the state! November 15, 1965, arrived, and the Disney brothers, along with Governor Burns, went to the table and provided some details at a press conference in Orlando announcing the plans.

The day after the press conference, the *New York Times* ran a piece that gave a broad overview of the project. They followed that piece up five days later with another, longer, article; let us have a look at both. From the article on the 16th:

> Walt Disney announced here today the purchase of 27,000 acres in Orange and Seminole Counties for the construction of a Disneyland-East. The use of anonymous buyers to acquire the land parcels made for one of the biggest mystery real estate transactions in Florida history.

> The site is about 12.5 miles southeast of Orlando and 35 miles as the crow flies from Cape Kennedy. The price was not disclosed, but Mr. Disney said that $70 million would be spent to build what he tentatively called "The City of Yesterday and the City of Tomorrow."

> The Governor estimated that the new Disneyland could account for a 50 percent increase in tourism and a substantial rise in state tax revenues. He noted that 15 million tourists had spent $3 billion in Florida last year.[37]

In February of 2016, Florida Governor Rick Scott said Florida had become the first state to welcome more than 105 million out-of-state and international tourists. Take a guess where this announcement was made. You guessed it—

Walt Disney World. The governor noted that obviously Orlando is critical to the state's success.

"Orlando is the most visited destination in the United States. It's the most visited city, and certainly the home of the theme park capital of the world, right? No place else on earth can compare to that."

In 2014, Orlando alone recorded sixty-two million visitors, which includes in-state, out-of-state, and international visitors. I'm sure Governor Burns would marvel at the influx of visitors to the state, due in large part to Disney.[38]

On November 21, 1965, after the country had a few days to digest the big news, here is the final article from the *New York Times*:

> Mr. Disney came here with his brother Roy, and ten executives of Disney Productions to meet with state and local officials. The amusement and educational center will not be called Disneyland, after its California counterpart. A possible name mentioned by Mr. Disney is Disney World.
>
> Among those who accompanied Mr. Disney to Orlando was Brig. Gen. William E. Potter, who was vice president of the New York World's Fair. He will be in charge of the Florida operation.
>
> According to Mr. Disney, the project will take about 18 months to plan and the same amount of time to implement it. He hopes to get underway by January, thus putting its opening early in 1969.
>
> Florida was selected over several other places in the eastern half of the country. "We have been considering for some time where we could place another Disney attraction. We have had offers from all over the world. We have even been offered free land in some areas, but we decided on Florida because of its year-round mild climate and the fact that it already has a large tourist volume.
>
> "We want this to be a family-style entertainment, as Disneyland in California is. It will not be merely a copy of what we have there, although we may bring to Florida some of the things

that have proved to be of great interest to our visitors in California.

"Of course, we have to make money to stay alive, but making money is the furthest from our thoughts in this new enterprise. I mean it. We want it to be a labor of love."

The purchase of 27,000 acres in Florida, he went on, was made to protect against an influx of honkytonk attractions and other undesirable businesses on the fringes of the new enterprise. Much of the land will serve only as a buffer zone.

When asked what type of things would be featured in the Florida attraction, Mr. Disney replied: "Frankly, I don't know. I have a lot of ideas buzzing in my head. After the first of the year, we will get our staff together and try to come up with certain plans. Certainly, the Florida attraction will have to be unique, something different from what we have in California. I am all keyed up about this, and we are ready to go to work as soon as some legal matters have been straightened out."[39]

Obviously, the project was still a bit uncertain in Walt's head, or at least that was what he was willing to divulge to the public. Over the next several months, Walt would come to refine his thoughts on the Florida Project, and members from Disney were meeting with officials from Florida to work out their master plan for the land—from a legal and municipal aspect.

Over the course of the next several months, stories would trickle out to the press about some of Walt's intentions. In late May of 1966, Walt was spotted in Rochester, New York. He flew in to get a tour of their Midtown Plaza, one of the first indoor shopping malls in an urban setting in the United States, which opened in 1962. Walt remarked that he was "quite impressed with your plaza, in the center of downtown. We're going to build a new community down there from nothing and we want to get it right." It was said that Walt was really impressed with the facility's high, wide ceiling, which gave a good feeling of openness.[40]

Interestingly, these quotes came from the local paper in Rochester, the *Democrat and Chronicle*, on Wednesday, May 25, 1966. Two days later, on Friday, May 27, 1966, the Associated Press ran a national story that noted that Walt hoped to put his Florida project under a roof and air condition it.

"It's the modern trend," said Disney. "I would have better control of the effects and illusions and you would have somewhere people could go when it rains, and of course you have heat and humidity."

Disney said his plans for the huge tourist attraction in central Florida were still not firm. He estimated it would be six months before he could give any details or set a date for starting construction. He figured his eventual expenses at $500 million, five times the figure mentioned when he first announced his intention to make Disneyland East.

"That's not much is it?" he asked reporters who gasped a bit at the figure. The subject of air conditioning was brought up by reporters, and Disney indicated he had no firm plans on that either. But he said: "The modern trend is to, even in shopping malls, have some kind of climate control. I'd like to put it under a roof. I wouldn't want anything you were conscious of. It would have to be right in keeping with what we're doing.

"Of course, we'd have to anchor it down so the hurricanes wouldn't blow it away." He said he did not have in mind a dome like the Astrodome in Houston. But he gave no other details.[41]

As the article stated, it would be about six months before he would release more details about the project. And by October 27, 1966, Walt was preparing to share his vision with the world. On this day, Walt filmed segments for his EPCOT film, which gave a detailed look at his dreams for the acreage he had bought down in Florida.

At last, this film would explain his Disney World concept, and, more specifically, reveal his groundbreaking and potentially society-changing Experimental Prototype Community of Tomorrow.

Just a few short days later, on November 2, 1966, Walt was admitted to St. Joseph's Hospital. The studio released the following statement:

> Walt Disney was initially admitted to the hospital on Nov. 2 for treatment and preliminary examination of an old polo injury. During the preliminary examination, a lesion was

discovered on his left lung. Surgery was decided upon and performed the next week. A tumor was found to have caused an abscess which, in the opinion of the doctors required a pneumonectomy. Within four to six weeks, Mr. Disney should be back on a full schedule. There is no reason to predict any recurrence of the problem or curtailment of his future activities.[42]

December 15, 1966

Walter Elias Disney passes away at St. Joseph Hospital at the age of 65 in Burbank, California.

To quote Jim Morrison, another iconic figure from the 1960s, albeit from the opposite end of the spectrum, "This is the end, beautiful friend."

As the press release implied, Walt never was able to resume his full-time duties at the studio, as the studio had suggested. Tragically, all his years of cigarette smoking had caught up with him. At the age of sixty-six, Walter Elias Disney passed away in the hospital at 9:35 a.m., his death attributed to acute circulatory collapse.[43]

That day in December 1966, the world lost not only an icon but also a revolutionary who had changed his world and the world for decades to come. Walt Disney is a once-in-a-lifetime personality. He changed things in our society on par with the icon of his day, Henry Ford, and an icon of our day, Steve Jobs.

During his time on this earth, Walt straddled yesterday, his day, and tomorrow, and with such greatness.

I once went to hear Marty Sklar speak (a legendary imagineer who worked at Walt's side), and he touched on having to write something for the press immediately after Walt passed away, it was a herculean task.

How does one eulogize Walt Disney? What an incredibly hard subject to narrate or encapsulate. So, for someone as insignificant as me in this "Disney story" to try to quantify his achievements and explain what Walt means, or meant to society, entertainment, childhood, vacationing—the list could go on and on, would almost be an exercise in futility, so I won't even attempt.

And truth be told, from the casual observer who happens to catch a Disney film on television, to the folks who return year after year to a Disney theme park, society as a whole already understands the greatness of Walt Disney.

As Disney is omnipresent in some part of our daily lives, which in turn all reaches back to our beloved Uncle Walt, Walt Disney's World truly is everywhere, not just in Florida.

Walt's death obviously sent shockwaves throughout the world. Aside from the millions and millions of adoring fans around the globe, Walt left behind two families: his immediate family—wife, daughters, grandchildren, and the like—and his studio family.

In the days following his death, several stories were published giving some insight into Walt's personal finances and how his estate would be divided. According to Walt's contract with Walt Disney Productions, he drew a salary of $182,000 a year and a deferred salary of $2,500 a week. Also, there were options to buy up to 25 percent interest in each of his live-action features. Walt began exercising some of these options starting in 1961.[43]

By 1964, the corporation that bore his name grossed $110 million, and Walt owned roughly 38 percent of the publicly traded company.[43] Additionally, there was the corporation RETLAW, (which is Walter spelled backward) which controlled the use of Walt's name commercially. Walt was the sole owner of this company—in 1981, Walt's family sold their interest in RETLAW to the Disney Company, along with the family-owned narrow-gauge steam railroad and monorail at Disneyland for $46.2 million in stock.[44]

Walt's will left his significant assets to three major trust funds. The first trust was the Disney Family Trust, with 45 percent of the estate going to his wife, Lillian; his two daughters; and his grandchildren.

The second trust, another 45 percent of his estate, went to the Disney Foundation. The will stated 5 percent of this was to remain in the foundation to be earmarked for charitable organizations at the discretion of the foundation. The remaining 95 percent of the second fund goes to the California Institute of the Arts, a university Walt helped create. The third and final trust went to Walt's three nieces and his sister.[45]

Clearly, on a financial level, Walt's family would be OK. But could the same be said for his studio family? Many wondered about the future of the studio. Walt had been the catalyst for nearly every creative endeavor, and with the massive Disney World project announced less than a year ago, could this project come to fruition?

A week after Walt's death, the answer was found in a newspaper article about the Florida Project. It was a resounding yes.[46]

Older brother Roy, who shunned the spotlight and really kept the Disney machine rolling financially, affording Walt the opportunity to unleash his creative fury upon the world, would step in and commandeer the ship—Roy really is an unsung hero all along in the entire Disney story, a remarkable and creative man in his own right.

The project would proceed, as the Disney legal teams were already working diligently to create the municipal corporations and framework for Disney to control their land in Florida. The unprecedented power Disney sought would need to be approved by the state of Florida before the project could commence.

According to a full-page article in the *Palm Beach Post* on February 12, 1967, Disney presented the Orange and Osceola County governments three acts for their approval. The first two acts were the same—the creation of two municipalities, the cities of Lake Buena Vista and Bay Lake.

The third act would be for the creation of the Reedy Creek Improvement District, which would encompass the entire Disney property. In its simplest form, these acts basically gave Disney complete power and control over their land. You name it—drainage, utilities, sewer systems, construction, public transportation, police, fire, and so forth.

In addition to control, the act had a provision allowing Disney to issue bonds to fund necessary improvements throughout their district.[47]

The explanation here is obviously the abridged version of the legalities of the project, as it is quite detailed, but you get the gist of it. Mickey had carte blanch over the land.

So why would Disney, need such unprecedented control over their land? Well, this is where the EPCOT film Walt created just two months before his death became important.

By February 1967, the Florida Project was still very much undefined to the public. There were ideas thrown about and blurbs in the media, but a definite plan had never been presented, as Walt passed away before this could happen.

On February 2, 1967, all of this changed, as Roy announced the company's plans, and the EPCOT film was finally revealed publicly in Orlando to nearly a thousand invited state lawmakers and leaders of the community.

And what did these folks get? Walt Disney in all of his glory, speaking passionately in one of his last and most important on-screen performances. After a long wait, what was finally coming to Florida? Let's have an overview from the *New York Times*:

> Walt Disney Productions today announced it would build the world's first glass-domed city in central Florida amid Disneyworld, a $100 million entertainment center. Disneyworld would be five times the size of Disneyland in Anaheim, California. The initial cost of the city was put at $75 million.
>
> Ending 15 months of speculation since the late Walt Disney bought 27,400 acres of land in Orange and Osceola Counties, Roy Disney, the 72-year-old heir to the control of his brother's entertainment empire outlined the project to businessmen and state officials and newsmen.
>
> Governor Claude Kirk watched a special film on the project and then predicted the 43 square mile development would be worth $6.6 billion in economic benefits to the state in 10 years. Disney officials said that except for roads, the center would not require a nickel of tax money or any tax concessions.
>
> Roy Disney said the entertainment portion could be opened within three years. The glass-domed city would take a quarter of a century to construct. No construction date has been set yet.
>
> The presentation, narrated by Walt Disney, who died December 15, was termed by Disney officials as "Walt's last film." It showed a 50-acre air-conditioned city of tomorrow

centered in a 1,000 acres industrial park between Orlando and Kissimmee. The city was called Epcot for experimental prototype community of tomorrow.

It will be a blueprint of a new city dedicated to the dream of America," Roy Disney said. "People will live as they cannot live anywhere in the world." Mr. Disney said the futuristic city would be laid out like a wheel, the hub containing a 30-story motel and convention center with stores, theaters, restaurants, nightclubs and office buildings.

He said it would have a completely closed environment with a minimum of traffic. "The pedestrian would be king," he said.

He said high-speed monorails would transport workers to the hub of the city from three outlying areas. Outside the central hub will lie areas of high-density apartments, green belt residential districts and low-density living areas. Once inside the city, workers will move on electric conveyor type cabs or "people movers" as Disney phrased it.

The audience was told after the showing of the film that the entertainment section of Disneyworld could open in the summer of 1970 if the company's legislative package is passed.[48]

Needless to say, the EPCOT film did its job, and on May 23, 1967, Claude R. Kirk, the thirty-sixth governor of Florida, gave Disney the keys to their kingdom by signing into legislation their requests creating the two towns and the overall improvement district.

With the all the *t*'s crossed and *i*'s dotted, it was time for Disney to get to work. Initial opening projections were for some time in 1970. However, there were still lots of dredging, land clearing, and even a few union labor strikes to persevere through before any significant progress could be seen on the property.[49] A revised date of January of 1971 seemed more appropriate. As the project trudged along, Disney refrained from putting an exact target on the project and merely suggested sometime during 1971.[50]

While the actual construction work progressed, Disney started to release dribs and drabs to the public about what to expect at Disneyworld.

On January 2, 1969, the newspaper *Florida Today* provided some new details about the project.

> A spokesman said this week, Disney "is not in a position right now to identify a specific opening date."

> Regardless, Disney World will open sometime in 1971 with its spectacular theme park, some five times larger than the present Disneyland in California. One departure from the California theme was noted by another Disney official, who said the site in Florida will be geared to "play and stay." He said the California park by virtue of its limited size, has been directed only to play.

> "But here you will be able to stay and play for a couple of weeks if you want," he added. There will be five or six massive Disney-operated hotels in the theme park. The actual themes of the resort living areas will include a south sea island village, a New England village, and an "Old West" village. The entire concept will be located adjacent to some 20 acres of man-made lagoon, now being clawed out by giant cranes and earth movers.[51]

Roughly two months later, on February 28, 1969, *Florida Today* ran another Disney World story, this time with a bit clearer picture and a few changes from the previous story.

> According to an SEC filing, Disney plans to sell $50 million in new bonds, convertible into Disney stock. Their new park would have "seven principle sections; Main Street, Liberty Square, Frontierland, Holidayland, Tomorrowland, Fantasyland, and Adventureland, with the seven "theme parks" being built on one side of a giant lake.

> Across the lake the corporation plans a village of hotels and motels, most built and operated by other companies that are now negotiating for contracts with Disney World. There will be golf, tennis, horseback riding, swimming, and sailing for hotel guests. The $165 million Disney investment does not include hotels and motels.

After the amusement park is in operation in 1971, Disney World plans to develop, on another section of the property an industrial park for light manufacturing and research.

Another phase of new development will have a model community of the future for both permanent and seasonal visitors. The prospectus says an airport big enough to handle jets is also in the long-range plans. There is no timetable for the construction to begin on the industrial park, airport, and model community.

Disney estimates that the new park will bring in eight million visitors a year.[52]

By September of 1969, enough progress had been made on the site that Disney was ready to commit to a date, October 1971. But as more and more information came out about the park, some folks in the press started to wonder, what happened to the City of Tomorrow?[53]

With everyone submerged in the creation of a bigger, better Disneyland, many forgot about the major project that had lit up Walt's face during the EPCOT film, the driving motivation of the Florida Project. According to a quote from Roy in November of 1969, EPCOT was still on the drawing board.

"Walt wanted this project, and he was particularly interested in Epcot," Roy Disney says. "Disneyland and the Magic Kingdom greatly involved him, of course, but I think that Epcot, a showcase new city, was really his greatest dream. That's my job now, to help it come true."[54]

But before Roy could even broach the subject of EPCOT, they needed to complete phase one, Disney World.

Walt Disney, Governor Burns, and Roy Disney on November 15, 1965, announcing their Florida Project. Courtesy of the Florida Memory Project.

February 2, 1967, Disney shows the EPCOT Film at a Winter Haven, Florida, movie theater. Photo courtesy of the Florida Memory Project.

CHAPTER FIVE

1970S

July 7, 1971

Ub Iwerks, the artist responsible for putting pencil to paper and creating Mickey Mouse, passes away at age 70.

Here is a name we didn't encounter much in the Disney story. Actually, we didn't see Ub at all, as we started after Mickey was created. But the book chronicling his life, *The Hand Behind the Mouse* (written by his granddaughter), is aptly named, and Ub was exactly that—the artist who animated everyone's favorite mouse.

Ub's story is an interesting one; his relationship with the Disney brothers went back long before the brothers barnstormed Hollywood with Mickey.

As the Disney legend goes, in the late 1920s Walt went to New York City to negotiate a better deal for the character his studio was producing, Oswald the Lucky Rabbit—the first few pages of this book show a few early advertisements for Walt's first critter. The negotiations didn't go so well. In fact, not only did he not receive the pay increase he was seeking, but he learned he didn't own the rights to the character. Walt lost Oswald and needed to start over with a new character. Thus, Mickey Mouse was born, and Ub Iwerks was the man to animate the mouse.[1]

After a whirlwind few years as the hand behind Mickey, Ub left the studio (Ub was actually a shareholder in the early days of the Disney studio) and went on to run his own animation studio. Eventually, Ub returned to Disney, where he settled in as a technical and engineering genius (he won two Academy Awards), not only for Disney productions but for some legendary films in Hollywood— he contributed to some scenes in the Alfred Hitchcock thriller *The Birds*.

Five years after Walt Disney died, another piece of Disney history and a major component of the original trio that created Mickey Mouse is now gone. Roy was now last man standing from that legendary threesome.

October 1, 1971

Walt Disney World opens in central Florida.

Four years, nine months, and sixteen days after Walt's death, the Vacation Kingdom within the sovereign state of Mickey Mouse was ready for business. As Roy O. Disney proclaimed in his Walt Disney World dedication speech, the park would be a tribute to his younger brother, Walter Elias Disney and therefore should be known as Walt Disney World (WDW), not merely Disney World.

Today we refer to the resort area that encompasses Magic Kingdom, EPCOT, Disney's Animal Kingdom, Disney's Hollywood Studios, and the surrounding water parks, shopping, hotels, and so forth, collectively, as WDW. But back in 1971, Walt Disney World was exclusively a theme park and two hotels, the Polynesian Village and the Contemporary. This was phase one of the broad plans that were Walt Disney World.[2]

All in all, Disney spent about $400 million to convert roughly 100 acres into the Magic Kingdom. The park's opening provided guests with a litany of Disney fun. Visitors spending the night could camp at the campgrounds or sleep in one of the two unique themed hotels. Just a quick trip on the monorail, and guests would find themselves at the theme park of their dreams.[2]

Similarly to today, a leisurely stroll down Main Street USA (which, as any rabid Disney fan will tell you, is actually the second floor, as ground level is the utilidor system that operates as the labyrinth of passageways for cast members to get around the park[3]) brings you to Cinderella's Castle and the hub that leads to what makes Disney, Disney. The numerous attractions featuring Audio-Animatronics performing in lifelike splendor all the Disney stories we know and love are spread throughout Adventureland, Frontierland, Liberty Square, Fantasyland, and Tomorrowland—paralleling Disneyland when it opened, with the exception of Liberty Square.

So what was the park like on the first day and the subsequent months? Was it an unfinished, unorganized, chaotic, hot mess like Disneyland? Well, not exactly, as Disney had learned from their mistakes and actually hoped for a small turnout. To foster this idea, the park debuted in October. This month was notoriously slow regarding tourism throughout the state of Florida.

Next, they didn't broadcast a live television program on the first day. The ninety-minute television special introducing the park to America aired on October 29, from 8:00 to 9:30 p.m. It featured Julie Andrews, Glenn Campbell, and a slew of other celebrities. This delayed program allowed the park to work out the kinks instead of having them captured on film for the world to see.[4]

Much like Disneyland's preview day, Disney relied on the press to spread the word about their new park. Leading up to and during the first days of the park, Disney ran press junkets in from all over the country to soak up WDW and report back to their hometown papers the delights of Walt Disney World. And to be quite honest, it was pretty uneventful. Surveying the stories of the day didn't yield much in the way of things remarkable.

But there are few interesting morsels from the first few days. Charles Ridgeway, the PR man for Disney, met with a group of reporters the night before. He informed them that the caravan out to the park was leaving at 4:30 a.m., as the park would open before 8:00 a.m., and he remarked that the exact number of guests arriving "could be anywhere from 10,000 to 80,000."[5] Boy, that was quite a wide number.

Well, it definitely wasn't 80,000. By midday, Donn Tatum, president of Walt Disney Productions, reported a head count of between 2,500 and 2,800 paid customers, remarking, "We're not disappointed by the turnout. It's just what we wanted."[6]

By day two, 11,115 guests visited the park.[7] A month and a half later, on November 26, 1971, WDW had their first attendance record with 55,000 people jamming the park, and park officials turned away an additional 3,000 cars.[8] Through January of 1972, just four months after opening day, over 2,000,000 people visited the park.[19]

Folks definitely marveled at the many aspects of Walt Disney World those first few days, from the gorgeous Polynesian Village hotel to the futuristic Contemporary Hotel, which allows the streamlined monorail to pass right through the building.

But the monorail was merely the start of the excitement. The real utopia of Walt Disney World is the Magic Kingdom. Feeling the excitement of those first few steps onto Main Street USA, affording all of us a glimmer of yesterday.

Then there's the journey to Cinderella's Castle, where the tough decision of which direction to proceed awaits you as the anticipation builds toward the thrill of immersing yourself into your first-ever Disney park attraction.

This is surely what visitors to the park on October 1, 1971, felt, but for most visitors to WDW (or, for that matter, Disneyland), one needn't be there for the opening day, as this scene plays itself out tens of thousands of times a day, even some forty years later. Whether it's visit 1 or 101, the magic and the excitement that are Disney truly transcend the decades.

One aspect of WDW that doesn't transcend the decades is the price. Long before the park hopper and Magic Bands, general admission on opening day was $3.50 for an adult; junior admission, ages twelve through seventeen, $2.50; and children three years through eleven, $1.00.[2] If you felt the need to bring man's best friend, your four-legged friend could stay at the WDW kennel for fifty cents a day, which included a lunch—for the dog, that is! [9] Individual attractions ranged from ten cents to ninety cents.[10]

There were even two package deals for the grand opening. The Family Fun Vacation package consisted of a three-day-and-two-night stay at one of the hotels, along with admission to the park for three guests and tickets for twenty-one attractions. The rates per person were $61.50 for an adult, $61.50 for a junior, and $23.50 per child. Single occupancy was $100.50.[2]

Then there was the Vacation Kingdom package, offering four days and three nights at one of the hotels, admission to the Magic Kingdom, and tickets for twenty-eight attractions. Rates were $90.00 per adult, $36.50 for a junior, and $35.50 per child. Single occupancy was $148.50.[2]

If a package deal wasn't to your liking, you could spend the night at the Polynesian Village or the Contemporary for $22.00 to $40.00 a night at either hotel. The Fort Wilderness Campsite was $11.00 for trailer sites, including hookup.[9]

One last look back at Walt Disney World from the days after the park opened is a quick story about the security force. It's from an article aptly titled "Magic Kingdom Police Make Only 'Nice Arrests.'"

Getting busted at Disney World is a gas. On opening day, Disney security guards went soft on three hooky-playing boys, forgave a runaway horse and admitted they try to make "nice arrests" of the more serious offenders. It is unlikely anyone will ever charge police brutality against these men wearing a badge pinned on colonial costumes, cowboy outfits, and Keystone Cop garb.

"It's the back corridor for all apprehensions," said security guard Dean Harrison. Harrison is the former probation officer of Livingston County near Rochester, N.Y.

"There are corridors behind all the attractions and shops that lead to the security office," said Harrison. In addition, Disney World's four-and-a-half acre basement includes streets which could be used to carry the prisoner away. A shoplifter could go into Cinderella's Castle with stolen merchandise under his coat and never be seen in the park again, for example.

The park has 200 security guards and not one has the power of arrest. "I'd talk with you about it if I saw you do something really wrong," said one guard. "I'd ask you to go with me, but I wouldn't touch you."

Security guards are instructed to "observe and report it" to their supervisor. When a really tough offender snubs his nose at the gentle security men, the supervisor will decide whether to notify the local sheriff or the Florida Highway Patrol.

"We've already been cased by the captains of shoplifting teams. They have captains that measure the counters and decide what merchandise they want. We're sure they were here in the two weeks before opening day," said Harrison.

Security guards are backed up by 20 to 30 plain-clothes men, but he said problems are few.

"Most people want to know where they can eat and where the restrooms are. I've only cautioned one guest to put his shirt on. There has been no other trouble. We're not police or fuzz. We're here to help guests."

The security guards are linked by a commercial network large enough to serve a town of 50,000, and it's going to be expanded.[8]

Well, there you have it: a little sliver of Disney security, circa 1971.

For the most part, the foundation of the Magic Kingdom in 1971 is by and large the same thing we can experience today. Sure, there have been quite a few additions and subtractions in the way of attractions.

Additionally, there have been updates and modifications to the lands of the park, and we will cover some of them as we encounter them over the next few chapters. But before we leave Walt Disney World, there is one more notable story tied to it.

This story comes from my "Discarded Disney" file. On Saturday, August 7, 1971, a story ran in the newspaper *Florida Today* (the paper covers Brevard County, which is to the east of Orlando and known as the Space Coast, as it is along the Atlantic and is home to Kennedy Space Center and Cape Canaveral) that said that while Disney was still sorting out their first month of Walt Disney World, they weren't sure what they were going to do with the beachfront property they had bought in Brevard County, something that was loosely termed Disney by the Sea.

Wait, what? There's more land? And this land is beachfront and over an hour away from WDW? Yep, that's precisely the case.

This article indicated Walt Disney Productions purchased several oceanfront tracts of land (roughly 92.17 acres, with 4,273 feet of ocean frontage, for $1.59 million) south of Melbourne Beach as an "ocean playground" for visitors to Walt Disney World.[11]

So here's what we know. In the 1971 and 1972 Walt Disney Productions annual report, the property is mentioned. The company said families visiting WDW would be able to "enjoy natural ocean beach playground" on their eighty acres of land south of Melbourne Beach. And officially that's really all you will ever hear from Disney about the property, other than some dribs and drabs in the newspapers over the next six years.[12]

In November of 1973, a newspaper article, again from *Florida Today*, indicated Disney did a partial land transfer for tax purposes. The transfer went from one Disney company to another, similar to how Disney had purchased land for

Walt Disney World under dummy corporations. The corporation name Disney used in this transaction was Compass Rose Corp.[13]

Then things were quiet for a few years. In May of 1978, some more details came to light from *Florida Today*, this time with direct quotes from Dick Nunis, then executive vice president of Walt Disney World.

> "Few places in the world offered us what we could buy in Brevard County. We needed and wanted a location close to Walt Disney World, and the fact that we could buy land with ocean on one side and river on the other was perfect."

> That was the way Dick Nunis described the thoughts of the entertainment company's top officials seven years ago as they set about—quietly at first—buying South Brevard mangroves and beachfront.

> But it will be quite some time, says Nunis, before Mickey Mouse will be smiling down on any tourists strolling along Brevard beaches or sailing the Indian River.

> "I can tell you, without evocation, that Walt Disney has nothing planned for that property for at least five years. That's not to say we have something planned after that point. We don't."

> Nunis said that Disney really never has gone past the planning stage for its Brevard property, or the "Disney by the Sea" project.

> "We have a concept in mind of what we want to do. We have put together some ideas but nothing is set for the future, that's for sure." Nunis said.

> Brevard, actually, was not Disney's first choice. Bob Foster, the man who engineered the land deals in this county for Disney, said the entertainment conglomerate was interested in property near New Smyrna Beach and the now-developed John's Island project in Indian River County. However, the land prices for the other parcels were not what Disney wanted to pay.

'The opportunity to expand. The opportunity to offer Walt Disney World visitors a complete Florida vacation, with a trip to the beach included, presented itself.

"We had the opportunity to acquire property in pristine beach area, and we didn't think it would there forever. So we started buying the land in Brevard," Foster said.

As early word leaked out about who was buying the land in south county, Brevardians were agog over tales about Disney building a monorail to link its entertainment park in Orlando within the county. There were stories about hotels, condominiums, marinas, underwater restaurants—all to be constructed on the Disney property.

"It makes me laugh now. Those stories were really something. I can say though we never had plans…never…to build a monorail. Can you imagine the problems? Environmental problems alone would be enough to stop us, notwithstanding the money involved.

"People think Disney has an endless supply of money. I wish we did, so we could do some of the things people ask of us." Nunis said.

He added that Disney's "concepts" which are tentative, at best, are to build condominiums and a "small" hotel on the property. A marina would be added that could handle sizable watercraft, and a restaurant has been planned, Nunis said.

He assessed that he could not offer too many specifics, especially on the cost of the "Disney by-the-Sea" project, partly because the planners at Disney are not sure what they have in mind.[14]

We obviously now know that "Disney by-the-Sea," never came to be. A real-estate transaction search with the Brevard County clerk in 2016 revealed the most recent transaction on a parcel of land held by Compass Rose Corp or Lake Buena Vista Properties was in 1998, when a small parcel of land was sold.

But Disney's preoccupation with oceanfront property in Florida didn't end with this discarded project. In fact, in October of 1995, Disney opened their

Vero Beach Resort, a mere two hours southeast of Walt Disney World.

The beach resort, which is part of the Disney Vacation Club, is themed around the Florida of yesterday. According to the press of the day, the creation of this resort was a shrewd business move, as "yearly polls of Disney World resort guests found that nearly half head to the beach before or after they visit the theme parks."[15]

December 20, 1971

Roy O. Disney passes away at seventy-eight years of age.

Just a mere eleven weeks after Roy Oliver Disney saw one component of his kid brother's final dreams come true, he passed away from a cerebral hemorrhage.

Roy was born June 24, 1893, making him eight years older than Walt. As the story goes from Roy's biography, *Building a Company* (page 46), he contributed the first $200 to give Walt his start. From his early days of operating the camera to keeping the books when it was a small-time operation, Roy was always there to provide support for his brother.

For the greater part of both of their lives, Roy brought financial stability to the big dreams Walt conjured up—regardless of cash flow or budget. Roy was a business maven for the Disney empire.

Roy was never one to look for the glory or notoriety of show business. He stayed in the shadow of his brother and operated, at times just as creatively as his brother, albeit in a different venue. Roy was able to cobble together business deals and secure funding, sometimes to his chagrin.

In January of 1964, Roy gave an interview to Bob Thomas, who covered Disney extensively for the Associated Press. Thomas also wrote a biography on both Walt and Roy. Here are a few quotes for the often interview-shy Roy.

> "Yes, it has been a very good year," said Roy Disney with characteristic understatement. From 1953 to 1964, gross income increased from $8 million to almost $82 million. Profits last year were at a record high of $6,574,000.

> As President and financial mind of the Disney empire, Roy leaves the spotlight to Walt. But in a rare interview, he discussed the partnership.

"He's a grand guy," said Roy of Walt. "It has always been a job keeping up with him. He gets the ideas, then I have to look at them from a practical prosaic view. Sometimes I've had to say no, and he'll accept it if he knows that my decision didn't come from lack of vision. There have been times when I just couldn't get the money.

"He's not a bad guy to work with. He knows what he wants and he'll listen to you—if you know what you're talking about. But if you're just shooting off your mouth, he won't hear a thing.

"My job is to help Walt do the things he wants to do," said Roy. "I deal with the banks and give Walt a free hand. The trouble with a lot of other movie companies is that the banks make decisions on the pictures."

Has the studio ever been in real trouble?

Roy smiled.

"We've always been pretty stretched out," he said. "Maybe that's why we've done so well—we always owed so much money. Only in the past three years have we been able to breath more easily.

"Product has always been our strength," Roy said. "It is the floor of our operation. The new money we get goes into the new product. If the time ever came when we got in financial trouble, all we would have to do is shut down new production and let the money roll in from what we already made."

As we all know, in the business world, money is everything. One can possess all the incredible dreams in the world, but without the capital to see them through, they are merely just that—dreams unrealized.

Through much of the Disney story, the brothers were undercapitalized. But despite this handicap, Roy's creativity and diligence helped Walt bring Mickey Mouse, animated full-length features, a television presence, and, of course, the Disney theme parks to the masses.

And in the end, his first business move was by far his best. By investing a couple of hundred dollars in his kid brother, decades later that investment was worth millions of dollars.

And do yourself a favor: check out Roy's biography by Bob Thomas, *Building a Company*. It gives Roy his due.

With that being said, on the opposite end of the spectrum, in what is probably one of *the* worst newspaper headlines I have ever seen (and believe me, after writing this book, composed predominantly of newspaper articles, I've certainly seen my share of headlines) the *New York Times* ran this headline to cover Roy's death: "Roy O. Disney, Aide of Cartoonist Brother, Dies at 78."[17]

Wow, aide of cartoonist brother? That's quite a lame title for a man who was integral in the Disney story. I mean, at least put down chairman of the board or CEO of the Disney Company. But perhaps that wasn't Roy anyway. Maybe he really was just his brother's right-hand man, two brothers with humble Midwest upbringings that changed the world.

In the days after Roy's death, executive changes were announced for Walt Disney Productions. Donn B. Tatum was elected chairman of the board and chief executive officer. E. Cardon Walker was announced as president and chief operating officer.[18]

Before Roy's death, Tatum was the president and Walker was executive vice president and chief operating officer.

March 22, 1975

Lake Buena Vista Shopping Village opens at Walt Disney World.

The shopping and dining extravaganza at WDW known today as Disney Springs has had several name changes over the decades.

While the area's identity has largely been the same—a place to spend your money without a price of admission—the area's name has changed quite a bit. Before it was Disney Springs, it was known as Downtown Disney (with an adjacent area called Pleasure Island, which for a hot minute back in 2010 was going to transform into something called Hyperion Wharf, which ended up in the discarded Disney file), and before it was Downtown Disney, it was called Disney Village Marketplace. And before that, it was called Walt Disney

World Village, and before that, it was known as Lake Buena Vista Shopping Village.

Despite the multitude of name changes and expansion over the decades, at its core, what appears today is by and large the same concept as Lake Buena Vista Shopping Village in 1975—waterfront shopping and dining.

The original incarnation of this area and some of the land adjacent to it was actually going to be something different, as in truer to the word "village."

With the success of WDW, in a January 1972 article in the *New York Times*, Disney announced they were going to build homes "to alleviate traffic" to the park. The original plan was to construct "a model residential-commercial community on 4,000 acres that could eventually move the corporation into national real-estate development.

"Designed as a 'second home' composed of condominiums and townhomes ranging in cost from $28,000 to $80,000, the community would incorporate features of a 'living environment' that would lessen the dependence on the automobile."[19]

By October of 1972, the plans were already underway for the housing sites.

> Lake Buena Vista, the already-started condominium town on the site bills itself as the "host community" to Walt Disney World. The project is the Disney organization's first, cautious attempt to try its hand at providing residential facilities, before it goes whole-hog with Epcot city.
>
> Lake Buena Vista's aim is more modest than Epcot's: it's merely a community of second homes for the wealthy, and a special attempt is being made to interest corporations in leasing houses as places to entertain clients. 80 homes, at prices ranging up to $100,000, will be occupied by November.
>
> The attached row-houses are generally arranged in clusters around golf courses, waterways and common green spaces.
>
> Disney will be "mini-Epcoting" some transportation experiments here; residents of Lake Buena Vista will be able to travel throughout the town via a system of electric carts and boats, and no automobiles will be necessary.[20]

As we've seen several times through the course of the book, what Disney announces isn't necessarily what Disney is going to create.

This became the situation with owning a home at Lake Buena Vista Village. By the time press started up again in late 1974 and early 1975 to announce the upcoming debut of the village, gone were any prospects of actually owning a home on Disney property.

Instead, when the village debuted, it was a waterfront European-style shopping village featuring twenty-nine shops and restaurants.[21]

Adjacent to the shopping center was a golf course, additional hotels, and an office building.[22] There would be no home ownership, but there were 133 one-, two-, and three-bedroom vacation villas, in addition to 32 tree-house villas, available to rent. From its opening day, the "village" was very successful, and, over the decades, it continues to be.[23]

The area evolved, and Disney revamped it when they deemed necessary or when the trends of the day have dictated, most notably when it came to food—wait, there wasn't a gluten-free and vegan bakery there in 1975, as there is today?

Regardless of the area's name or the wares the merchants are peddling, it is still an excellent place to enjoy away from the parks, and, best of all, it doesn't cost $100 to visit!

November 18, 1978

Mickey Mouse is a half century old!

Before the close of the decade, the mouse that started it all celebrated his fiftieth birthday in typical Disney fashion—with a television special on NBC.

The face that launched a thousand products (and billions of dollars!), one of the most recognizable, if not *the* most recognizable, faces in the world, actually looks a bit different than he did during his big screen premiere in 1928.

In 1979, Harvard University professor Stephen Jay Gould analyzed Mickey's features over the decades and published a scientific paper on the subject in an issue of *Natural History*. The article in its entirety is on thedisneystory.com, but here are few interesting observations from Dr. Gould.

The original Mickey Mouse was a rambunctious, even sadistic fellow. In their screen debut in *Steamboat Willie*, Mickey and Minnie pummeled, squeezed and twisted animals on a steamboat to produce a chorus of "Turkey in the Straw."

As Mickey became increasingly popular—indeed a national symbol—his behavior became more and more benign. And as he became more profitable, his appearance changed subtly but distinctly to match his new image.

While Mickey's chronological age never altered, his appearance became more and more baby-like. This change in appearance at a constant age is a true evolutionary transformation. Progressive juvenilization as an evolutionary phenomenon is called neotony.

Even if the Disney artists were not conscious of it, the underlying reason for transforming Mickey must have been to exploit the strong human feeling of affection for the young.

The tendency to view with affection animals such as chipmunks, rabbits and robins has nothing to do with their behavior, but stems from the fact that their head shapes and large eyes are reminiscent of a human baby.

A newborn child possesses a relatively large head attached to a medium sized body, with diminutive legs and feet.

Human eyes appear huge in the baby and relatively smaller as the child grows. The baby has a small chin and bulbous cranium that give way to a more slanted lower-browed head and a heavier, more pronounced jaw. Mickey Mouse has just the reverse evolution.

The Disney artists transformed Mickey in clever silence, often using suggestive devices that mimic nature's own changes by different routes.

To give him the shorter pudgier legs of youth, they lowered his pants and covered his spindly legs with a baggy outfit. His head grew gradually larger and while its original circular shape could not be changed unobtrusively, it was given the bulbous cranium of early childhood by the device of moving Mickey's ears back.[24]

A very interesting examination of Mickey over the years. In Gould's article "A Biological Homage to Mickey Mouse," he included an illustration of Mickey Mouse over fifty years, which clearly exhibits the detailed research he presented. Mickey's eye size increased from 27 percent of head length to 42 percent of head length.[24] Apparently Walt and his boys at the studio not only mastered animation and the marketing of their products, but they dabbled in psychology as well!

Well, here we are at the end of another decade. The opening of Walt Disney World made for an exciting and fruitful decade of Disney. Despite losing their cofounder, a new Disney legacy was born in Florida.

Even before WDW opened in October of '71, Disney was thriving financially. In February of 1971, their stock hit an all-time high price of $175 a share (the stock closed at $69 a share on the day Walt died, just five years earlier).[25]

On the studio side of the company, the hit movies *The Love Bug*, *The Jungle Book*, and *The Aristocats* from the late sixties and early seventies set the stage for a very profitable start to the seventies.

As the decade progressed, theme park attendance on both coasts held strong. By mid-decade, attendance numbers were buoyed when a little ride named Space Mountain debuted at Disneyland in 1977 and WDW in 1975—even former astronaut Gordon Cooper gave the attraction a ringing endorsement. Gordon said, "It's about as close as you can safely get to actually being in space."[26] Of course, Astronaut Cooper was employed by Disney at the time as a VP at WED.

But as the decade inched along, even a "realistic" trip to outer space couldn't stave off some looming trouble. By 1978, plans were in the works for not one but two new Disney theme parks for the 1980s. However, things on the studio side of the company were starting to look unstable.

In 1971, Disney optioned the rights to the story *The Chronicles of Prydain*. They were going to use the book loosely to create the full-length feature *The Black Cauldron*.

By 1978, the film was already four years behind schedule. Disney pushed the film's release back to 1980, and, as that date got closer, it was pushed again to 1984. The film was finally released in 1985.

So what held up production on this movie? Talent, or lack thereof. Apparently, Disney had trouble finding animators who could handle their productions.

In 1972, animating legend Eric Larson started a talent search to replenish the pool of animators for the studio. His results were less than thrilling.

> "We'd like 30 good animators," he said. He looked at thousands of portfolios and tried out 100 young animators in the last six years. Of those, 35 remain; and only 16 are in animation. "When someone is hired, you can't tell how good he'll be," Mr. Larson said. "Animation is limited only by imagination and the ability to draw what you can imagine.
>
> "People come here with master's degrees in art and they can't draw worth a damn. Art teachers are interested in static figure drawing. We deal with weight, action, movement. You have to be able to draw the relationship of a character's coat to the rest of his body or the relationship of his cuffs to the rest of his coat."[27]

Sort of sounds like some of those early comments from Walt during the mid-1930s when he was looking for talent to produce *Snow White*. The only difference here is that Walt's labor situation had a much better outcome.

Roughly a year after Eric Larson gave this interview, eleven animators abruptly quit the studio, in September of 1979. This caused a delay to the release of another film, *The Fox and the Hound.*

This time period was actually the beginning of some dark days for the studio. Financially, things were still very prosperous; 1978's earnings saw $98.4 million in profit on $741.1 million dollars.[28] But outside the theme parks and inside the studio, life after Walt and Roy was starting to seem turbulent.

Could the realization of EPCOT and the return of a Disney family member to the helm of the corporation right the ship, or would Disney free-fall during the 1980s?

CHAPTER SIX

1980S

October 1, 1982

EPCOT Center opens at Walt Disney World.

A decade and a year after Walt Disney World opened, Disney pulled back the curtain on EPCOT. Unfortunately, the original dream that was to be EPCOT, the futuristic city of tomorrow, where Walt planned to reengineer and revitalize the cities of today, all but died with him, and then eventually with Roy.

Details about the park trickled out to the press years before construction even commenced. The project was still being presented with a few generalized components of Walt's EPCOT, sans the housing. The park mainly centered on technology and its role in our future—with a smattering of that Disney nostalgia for yesterday and an altogether new twist.

Before Disney broke ground for EPCOT Center in October of 1979, here is how the company envisioned the project in March of 1977, from an interview given to the press.

> The future…it's happening now. The total concept: EPCOT, an Experimental Prototype Community of Tomorrow, billed as "an international forum for creative ideas and technologies." The site: the heart of Walt Disney World's 27,400 acres.
>
> EPCOT will feature Future World, a dream of the late Walt Disney, which will gather predictions from top minds and mold workable, logical, very possible scenarios of future technology's impact on a variety of fields.
>
> Rod Madden, Walt Disney World's publicist, when asked what Future World will entail replied "Let your mind go. Imagine what life will be like in 50 or 100 years."

AARON H. GOLDBERG

While the entire concept has not been detailed, the theme has been settled upon. "Man and his Spaceship Earth," which will serve as a framework into which specific plans will be laid.

Basically, Madden foresees an introduction to the future through a one-of-a kind combination of film and automated techniques to launch visitors into the complex. From there, he said, avenues will lead off into specific areas touching on the future world of health and medicine, agriculture, communication, oceanography, space, nutrition and transportation. He said they may even have a typical household for the year 2030 and experimental dwellings.

"He (Walt Disney) wanted to be able to change as technology changed. You may come to EPCOT in 1985 and come back five years later and see nothing you saw before," said Madden.

Although rumors circulating within the Orlando community have led some to believe that EPCOT will offer actual residences of the future to interested area people, Madden said this is not the case. While he said it is a possible option that experimental dwellings may be tested by actual live-in families for a short period of time, he pointed out that the performance of a residential community would defeat the purpose in the fluid Future World concept. "We believe," said Card Walker, president of Walt Disney Productions, "that to achieve Walt Disney's goals for EPCOT, we must avoid building a traditional community, but seek to communicate and demonstrate practical ways of improving the environment for living."[1]

In addition to the technology of tomorrow, EPCOT would be home to many lands. Not the lands of the Magic Kingdom, like Fantasy or Tomorrow, but the lands of the earth, showing the cultures and iconic landmarks of the world, via the World Showcase. Quoting from the same article:

The sister seed in the EPCOT pod is pledged to provide to all nations an international forum for their countries color and culture and to provide visitors, what will amount to a trip around the world.

Designers have been working up ideas for pavilions, each
including a high capacity adventure enabling guests to "travel
through the heart of the nations." According to Madden,
while no contracts have been signed yet, a half a dozen major
countries are expected to sign in the next few months and
some 30 nations are said to be interested.

Germany, a bloc of Arab nations, Venezuela, Mexico, and
Japan are among those in the advanced stages of planning
pavilions. Madden reports several US companies are now
scrutinizing plans for their participation in the US pavilion.

On the drawing board for Germany, according to Madden is
a Rhine River cruise which will explore the sights along the
fabled river; for Venezuela a trip on an authentic "teleferico"
or cable car, through the nation's heritage in search of the
legendary "El Dorado" or City of Gold, and for Japan
traditional Kabuki dinner-show or an experience similar to a
walk on the famous Ginza.[1]

Four years after this article, EPCOT Center was by and large just what this
article outlined—two themed lands with a lake dividing the regions. Visitors
wouldn't get to experience life entirely submerged in a new environment, with
futuristic or novel undertones. But they would get to experience a taste of
technology to come and enjoy a stroll around some replica countries. And
despite the grand projections set forth by Walt Disney in 1966, what came to
be EPCOT Center was still a feeling of pride for the company.

Disney officials say EPCOT represents the concepts Walt
Disney espoused—a place to show off new ideas and
emphasize technologies. "It doesn't necessarily have to be a
city where people live permanently," adds Charles Ridgeway, a
Disney spokesman.

"Everyone has his own idea of what Walt meant. And
EPCOT has the potential to accomplish what he had in mind.
I don't think anyone feels ashamed at what we've done. On
the contrary."[2]

Marty Sklar gave a bit more information about the park in an article from the
New York Times a week before the park opened.

One of the major sections is Future World, a six-pavilion presentation on scientific developments in communications, energy, transportation, agriculture, and imagination.

World Showcase, the other major thematic section, traces the architectural, social and cultural heritages of nine nations: China, Canada, Japan, Mexico, Italy, Germany, France, the United Kingdom and the United States.

"I can't say that Walt wouldn't have carried that original concept off, but it may have changed," said Martin A. Sklar, the center's chief architect and a 28-year associate of Disney Enterprises.

Cost became a major factor along the way, and Disney's death in 1966 also dampened enthusiasm. In more recent years, Disney associates have said in a tone of humor that their boss may not have been able to develop a sense of cohesiveness within his community as he had been able to develop with his cartoon characters.

"So in looking at this in light of developments after we've built Disney World here, we said wouldn't it be more effective if we could create a series of turn-ons that people could take back to their own communities," Mr. Sklar said in explaining the approach to Epcot.

Mr. Sklar, vice president for creative development of WED Enterprises, an arm of Disney Productions, said the nearly three-year construction job was preceded by nearly five years of research and consultations with companies, countries and individuals considered leaders in their field.

"We knew from the beginning that no one could do this alone, we had to involve companies and countries for two reasons," said Mr. Sklar. "We needed the capital and if we could blend their knowledge with ours, the park would become more credible. It was important because this was the first time we weren't dealing with fantasy."

While Disney Productions has provided the bulk of the financing for the Epcot Center, companies have agreed to pay $300 million over a 10-year period as sponsors for the various pavilions and agreed to give near-total control of quality and conceptual presentation of their pavilions to Disney.

Among the American companies involved are the Bell Telephone System, the Exxon Corporation, the General Motors Corporation, Kraft Inc., Sperry Univac, the Eastman Kodak Company, the American Express Company and the Coca-Cola Company.

Officials said that Time Inc. withdrew because of a difference over approach to a pavilion and that no sponsor had been found for a site, the Living Sea, slated to open in 1984.

In most instances, the sponsoring companies will receive some benefit. For example, only Coca-Cola's soft drinks will be sold at the park.

Next year, when major construction is scheduled to be completed, the General Electric Company's pavilion is expected to open, and Disney officials say they hope to add three other areas to the World Showcase, including Israel, Equatorial Africa, and Spain.[3]

Disney followed the schematic they had used during the opening of the Magic Kingdom at WDW: rely on the press to get the word out, implement a "soft opening" during the slow tourism month of October, and, finally, cap the first month off with a television special.

Let's have a look at each of these aspects during EPCOT Center's grand opening.

Local and national reporters descended on EPCOT Center for the press preview of the park. *The Lakeland Ledger* was one of the papers on-site to chronicle the park for their readers.

When Disney's $400 million Magic Kingdom opened its doors 11 years ago Friday, the nation's press was there. But Friday, when Epcot opened, the press was there in force.

"We've got about 150 press people here," said Charlie Ridgeway, press coordinator for the opening. Ridgeway, who was at Disney for the Magic Kingdom opening, said that's "at least double, or maybe triple" the number of reporters there for the 1971 opening.

In all, 19 radio stations broadcast programs from locations throughout Epcot. "I think when we opened the Magic Kingdom, not many people in the news media thought we were talking about something the size we were talking about," said Ridgeway. "This time, they knew we were serious. That's why there's an increase in coverage."

Eleven years ago, few television stations were equipped for live coverage or "instant" cameras to relay pictures quickly back to the local station. Friday, many of those cameras were evident.

Reporters noticed a deviation from past Disney policy—the company has never sold alcoholic beverages in the Magic Kingdom. But wine, beer and mixed drinks are available at theme restaurants in Epcot.

Ridgeway downplayed the introduction of alcohol. "All the time, liquor has been available at the Contemporary and Polynesian hotels, just outside the Magic Kingdom and nobody's made a big point out of that," said Ridgeway. "We don't have it in the Magic Kingdom, because there are many things there for children."

Some things never change, and standing in line—for both exhibits and food—has long been standard practice at Disney World. Ridgeway said the restaurants at Epcot will not take reservations, but if a prospective diner appears in person the guest can get a seating time.[4]

Take-home point about EPCOT from this reporter: yes, finally some booze at WDW!

Well, alcohol or no alcohol, EPCOT's first month was a success. There were a few bumps in the road with long lines and some issues with food service, but, all in all, the attendance numbers painted a picture of success.

Although Disney doesn't like to release exact attendance figures observers estimated that at least 25,000 people thronged through the 260-acre attraction when it opened for business—more than two and a half times the number some executives had anticipated.

In all, about 1 million people had visited the Walt Disney World complex—the Magic Kingdom and Epcot Center—since the doors were opened to the public Oct. 1. This indicates that Epcot had drawn about 650,000 guests in its 24 days in existence, and the Magic Kingdom about 350,000. The Magic Kingdom usually draws just under 15,000 people a day in October, Disney publicist Charles Ridgeway said.[5]

"Epcot is a success without a doubt," said Disney chairman Card Walker. But there were a number of technological breakdowns in some of the ride-through attractions, including Spaceship Earth, the central theme at Epcot's entrance and the Energy Pavilion.

There were also complaints by visitors of long lines at eating places and gripes by some that there were not enough dining spots or enough food. "The food industry is a very difficult business," said Dick Nunis, president of Disney's outdoor recreation division.

"We will evaluate the situation thoroughly, add eating places if necessary and we will improve."

'Sure, we're going to have problems, but we're going to solve them," said Walker about the mechanical glitches and food problems.

But it wasn't all bumps in the road; there were the usual Disney pageantry and pomp and circumstance. Quoting from the same article,

One thousand homing pigeons and multi-colored balloons fluttered into the sunny skies above an 18 story silver geosphere as Governor Graham joined Walker and the official "first family" of visitors in outdoor ceremonies at Epcot's entrance.

Rooftop trumpeters heralded the occasion. A Goodyear blimp hovered above the continuous stream of cars, and the monorail rolled silently overhead bringing crowds of visitors from the Magic Kingdom some three miles away.

"Epcot is a showplace dedicated to entertainment with a purpose," said Walker, who started with the company 45 years ago along with its namesake founder. "We want to entertain, to inform and to inspire all who come here."

Walker said Epcot was the culmination of 25 million hours of effort by thousands of people "propelled by the power and force of an idea of one man—Walt Disney."

The basic price of admission to Epcot is $12 for children 3 to 11, $14 for teenagers and $15 for adults 19 and over—but Disney officials encourage people to buy more expensive packages to see all its attractions. Children 2 and under get in free.[6]

Disney ramped up their grand opening festivities for EPCOT. There wasn't just one day to welcome EPCOT to the Disney theme park portfolio, as over the course of the month, EPCOT would feature prominently in the news. There was the "soft" opening day on October 1, then there was the television special, and, of course, there was the official opening ceremony on October 24, 1982, which featured invited guests—President Ronald Reagan was invited but was unable to attend. One prominent guest who was there was Lillian Disney, Walt's widow.

Lillian watched over the celebration and gazed upon the International Ceremony of the Waters and dedication of Fountain of Nations in Future World. This ceremony featured cultural representatives from 29 nations who traveled to Epcot to pour water from their nation into Epcot's Fountain.[7]

Another promotional event centering around the World Showcase took place on October 18. It wasn't located at the park but at the Orlando Airport.

For the first time in history, two supersonic airplanes known as the Concorde touched down within a split second of each other.

One plane was from British Airways and the other from Air France—both companies were sponsors of pavilions at EPCOT's World Showcase.

The two planes typically only flew into New York or Washington, DC, but due to their involvement at EPCOT, Disney arranged for both planes to touch down simultaneously in Orlando, an event over 35,000 went to witness live.[8]

Well, there you have it: the EPCOT we know and love (or tolerate, depending on your theme park desires). No, it isn't the EPCOT Walt spoke passionately about, and, in many ways, the original concept that was EPCOT still lingers and overshadows the park—perhaps more so during its early years. But for many, it is still interesting to ponder the initial concept and think about what it could have been or how it could have affected our future cities.

But the looming specter of Walt's dreams, his death, and what came to fruition does often cast a negative shadow over the park, most notably today. Many gripe that Future World isn't very futuristic, and some of those gripes may be valid. But for the better part of the first decade, many of EPCOT's presentations throughout Future World were not only futuristic but realistic.

The computer was a large part of Future World, and, as hard as it is for us to imagine today, these funky things weren't in every household or every person's pants pocket. For many, a visit to EPCOT was their first exposure to a computer.

The EPCOT prophecy in many ways has worked its way into our everyday life. A visit to Communicore (now known as Innoventions) behind Spaceship Earth in the early eighties was very computercentric, most notably with The Earth Station.

The Earth Station, sponsored by Bell Telephone, was a high-tech information and reservation system that featured touch-screen computers and two-way video guest-relations assistance—the EPCOT version of an iPhone and FaceTime circa 1981.

A quick stroll out of Communicore takes us over to the Universe of Energy Pavilion (now home to Ellen's Energy Adventure), which prominently features a technology we see today in just about any residential neighborhood: solar panels adorning the roof.

The pavilion debuted with eighty thousand three-inch wafer-shaped solar collectors arranged diagonally in 2,200 solar panels, capable of generating seventy-seven kilowatts of direct current that were then used to power the pavilion's ride vehicles.

These two examples aside, Disney's fascination with technology is still very prominent within the company—it just transcends EPCOT and the viewing public.

Disney Research, "the Science Behind the Magic," is the company's division that operates prominent research labs throughout the world. As their website states:

> Disney Research is an international network of research labs, with the mission to push the scientific and technological forefront of innovation at The Walt Disney Company.
>
> Disney Research combines the best of academia and industry, by doing both basic and application-driven research. We view publication as a principal mechanism for quality control and encourage engagement with the global research community.
>
> Our research applications are experienced by millions of people. We honor Walt Disney's legacy by innovating and deploying our innovations on a global scale.[9]

Their website highlights some of the remarkable technology they are developing that not only finds its way into the parks, but into society in general. Remarkable, almost sci-fi-sounding stuff is coming from their labs in California, Pennsylvania, and Switzerland.

The other component of Walt's EPCOT was obviously mentioned numerous times: the societal or housing experiment. And to a certain degree, this aspect was fulfilled—however, with a different target audience and a bit out of necessity.

As early as 1975, Disney remarked about their World Showcase being staffed by cultural representatives of each country.

> To assure that "appropriate social and cultural styles are maintained," Disney officials said that the pavilions of nations in the World Showcase would be staffed by cultural exchange students and former nationals.

Disney president Card Walker elaborated on that aspect of the World Showcase in an interview from July of 1975.

Disney president E. Cardon Walker described the World Showcase as sort of a permanent international exposition "where the nations of the world come together to present their culture and history, their tourism and trade opportunities in a people to people exchange." He said 10 to 30 nations eventually may occupy pavilions in the World Showcase.

"Supporting the world showcase will be EPCOT's international village where the young people who will operate the pavilions for participating nations will live and play and learn together during their time in America." Walker said.

"We hope that the nations of the world will send their young future leaders to operate the world showcase and build a base for international understanding for the years to come."[10]

And send their young people to Disney is exactly what these foreign countries did. As we know today, the World Showcase basically stands as it was described in the mid-1970s.

Each pavilion features the culture, cuisine, architecture, and friendly faces of that country.

Disney staffs the World Showcase (and to an extent some other areas of Disneyland and WDW) via their Cultural Representative Program.

As Card Walker noted, acceptance into the program allows young folks from the countries represented in the World Showcase to come live in America for one year and work at the World Showcase. Disney touts the program to prospective applicants as a way to not only earn money, but experience working and living the Disney way. Those accepted into the Cultural Representative Program will not only work in EPCOT but will live in Disney housing with others from the program.

As their website touts, "Whether you're assigned to a one, two, three or four-bedroom apartment, you'll share a bedroom with one or two Disney International Programs participants. Often times, your roommate(s) will be from another country, allowing you to learn about other cultures as you share your own. In addition, you'll improve your communication skills by being immersed in an English-speaking environment. You'll also learn about guest services directly from the company that's showing the world how it's done."

Now, EPCOT may not have revolutionized the way we live, but this little slice of the World Showcase has been providing monumental change and opportunity to tens of thousands of folks from foreign countries over the years. The program even carved its own niche in labor law and laws regarding foreign-exchange employment.

Disney lobbied and had the government create a new visa, the Q visa, or what is known as the Disney Visa. This visa was created exclusively for Disney with the specific purpose of staffing the World Showcase at EPCOT.

The visa isn't a generalized work permit or a cultural exchange permit, known as the J visa. The Disney visa is specific to working in the sense of a cultural exchange program.

Direct from the legislation: "The international worker would, as part of his employment, share the history, culture, and traditions of the country of the alien's nationality."[11]

The Disney visa was signed into law on November 29, 1990, by President George Bush as part of the Immigration Act of 1990.

In recent years, Epcot isn't the only user of the Q visa. The visa is now being used to attract future cast members from Sub-Saharan Africa, Asia, and Brazil. The workers from Africa and Asia are being utilized throughout Disney's Animal Kingdom Lodge and the Animal Kingdom Park.

Collectively, the Disney Visa and International College Program is not without controversy from some (mainly those claiming Disney gets cheap labor), and it has others applauding the opportunity given to young people from all over the world to not only become a part of America and the culture but to experience Disney in all its glory. Perhaps it's a symbiotic relationship with both sides benefiting, depending on your viewpoint.

So what really is EPCOT? As the quote said earlier, EPCOT is many things to many people. On the surface it's a half a handful of the future from Future World (at least for the decade or so after EPCOT debuted) and eleven handfuls of worldly culture via the World Showcase, spread over three hundred acres at the price of nearly $1 billion just a few miles from the Magic Kingdom.

The park is certainly unique among all the Disney parks. There is very little fantasy, and many feel it's more of an adult-centric park—that argument could probably be made more so in the early days, when Mickey and his peers didn't even roam the park greeting guests.

But today, with huge attractions like Test Track and Soarin, there is something for everyone. And, if nothing else, for many adults there is the mile-long stretch that numbs some of the Disney park madness and cultivates inebriation—the World Showcase!

April 15, 1983

Tokyo Disneyland, the first Disney theme park not on American soil, debuts.

Disney was getting good at building theme parks—three parks in roughly thirteen years. Not even a year after EPCOT showed the world their version of Japan at the World Showcase, Japan got to show the world their version of Disney.

In 1962, Chiharu Kawasaki, the first president of a Japanese-based development company, Oriental Land, visited Disneyland and told Roy Disney that he wanted to bring Disneyland to Japan. Through the sixties and seventies, it was estimated that roughly two hundred thousand visitors annually to Disneyland in California were coming from Japan, so a park in Japan seemed like a solid business venture.[12]

By 1974 the prospect of giving Mikki Mausu (Mickey Mouse) a home in Japan inched closer to reality. Disney was in discussions with the Oriental Land Company to bring Disney to the Land of the Rising Sun. By the end of 1978, it was all but a done deal. The *New York Times* from December 2, 1978, provided an outline of the business dealings.

> The project will be a joint venture between Disney Productions and two Japanese companies—the Mitsui Real Estate Development Company and the Keisei Electric Railway Company. Both Japanese companies hold equal shares in total ownership of Oriental Land.
>
> Disney Productions has announced that it will take a 10 percent equity share in the joint company.
>
> The $300 million cost of construction will be met almost entirely by Japanese interests. One-third will come from Mitsui,

Keisei and Oriental Land, another third from a consortium of
Japanese banks led by the Mitsui Trust and Banking Company,
and the remainder from a number of Japanese companies,
including the Bridgestone Tire Company, the Coca-Cola
Company Japan, and the Matsushita Electrical Industrial
Company, that will in return receive Tokyo Disneyland
trademark rights.

Yukihiro Nagaki, director of public relations at Keisei
Electric Railway, acknowledged that Japanese promoters are
still haggling with Disney Productions over certain royalty
payments. For example, he says: "Disney wants a rather large
sum for the use of their trademark on cigarette packages. But
we can't pay this amount because cigarettes in Japan are sold
by the government tobacco monopoly at regulated prices."[13]

In March of 1983, a month before the park's grand opening, the two sides
must have come to an agreement about having Mickey's mug on a pack of
Japanese smokes, as Disney Productions not only struck a royalty deal for the
park—10 percent on ticket sales and 5 percent on sales of souvenirs, food,
and beverages—but their interest in the park helped ensure that a syndicate
of seventeen Japanese banks would underwrite a loan of $63 million to Walt
Disney Productions.

The proceeds of the loan were going to be used for EPCOT and also served as
a hedge for yen payments that Disney expected to receive in royalty payments
for Tokyo Disneyland. The ten-year loan carried a fixed rate of 8.6 percent
interest, a much cheaper rate than Disney could have received stateside[14]—Roy
Disney would have been proud of that crafty business move!

Now that all of the disputes regarding cigarettes and yen were behind them,
Oriental Land got to work on their park. Construction costs ran over, way over
their original estimates of $300 million. When it was all said and done, the park
came in at $650 million and is a near replica in looks and layout of the parks in
California and Florida, with a few minor changes.

Oriental Lands' investment proved successful. The park's attendance the first
year grew steadily, and by August, just five months after it opened, Tokyo
Disneyland saw its first single-day attendance record, with 94,378 guests
arriving to greet Mikki Mausu.[15]

By 2013, Tokyo Disneyland's attendance was still holding strong—in fact, thriving. Their attendance grew by 15.9 percent, eclipsing 17.2 million visitors and becoming the second-most popular theme park in the world, behind WDW's Magic Kingdom.[16]

Oh, and if you thought only the common folk of Japan loved Disney, think again. When Japanese Emperor Hirohito passed away in February of 1989, he was buried with many of his most treasured mementos: a microscope, a list of his favorite sumo wrestlers, and the Mickey Mouse watch he was presented during his visit to Disneyland in the early 1970s.[17]

April 18, 1983

The Disney Channel debuts on cable television.

In November of 1981, Walt Disney Productions announced plans for a sixteen-hour-a-day cable television service.

Less than two years later, Mickey was on the air with a permanent home on cable TV, a premium channel most viewers at home needed to pay extra to receive.[18]

Despite the extra cost for the channel, subscribers grew steadily. From 1984 through 1992, subscribers went from 1.7 million to 7.1 million.[19]

As television and programming evolved through the 1990s and early 2000s, so did the Disney Channel.

Today there are multiple flavors of the Disney Channel, with Disney XD and Disney Junior. But the original channel is still the biggest draw, with 82.7 percent of homes in this country receiving the network.[20]

September 23, 1984

Michael Eisner becomes chairman of Walt Disney Productions.

As we just saw, the early 1980s were ripe with theme-park success for the Disney Company. Aside from the opening of EPCOT and the licensing agreement, which brought a Disney park presence to Japan, even Disneyland, got a makeover in May of 1983 with a redesign to Fantasyland.

However, as well as things were going on the theme park side of the business, things were equally disastrous on the studio side. The company was obviously still experiencing a creativity and production "hangover" two decades after their creative catalyst passed away.

Walt's flair and ingenuity for capturing an audience on the big screen wasn't something any executive could muster up. It had been Walt's gift, an instinctive and intuitive trait that was part of the fabric of what made Walt Disney, Walt Disney.

Over the course of his decades in Hollywood, he had crafted classic after timeless classic across several entertainment mediums. In the years after his death, not only could his studio not produce a timeless classic, they had trouble merely producing a hit or highly profitable movie.

We saw examples of this in the last chapter with the production of *The Black Caldron* and the exodus of talent during this time.

The issues that plagued the studio weren't just a single movie here or there. It was multiple movies. Disney strayed from animation and went into live action and comedies—after the hit of the movie, *The Love Bug* in 1968, they went back to that well three more times through the 1980s! What happened to Walt's theory of not doing sequels?

But it wasn't just sequels that disappointed Disney and eventually their audience. The studio put together a few movies with big-name Hollywood talent. *The Devil and Max Devlin*, starring Bill Cosby and Elliott Gould, flopped, as did *Popeye*, *Dragonslayer*, and *Watcher in the Woods*, to recount just a few.[21]

The studio committed big money to these films, and, in turn, they became big losses. There was even an article in the *New York Times* indicating that *TRON* could be flop as well, back in 1982.

It seems Disney held a screening for securities market analysts to preview the movie. After they viewed it, a few advised their clients to sell their holdings in Disney, as the movie was "seriously flawed" and had a "disjointed story."

The next day, Disney stock dropped $2.50 a share and then to $1.25 the day after that. As Disney senior vice president of finance Mike Bagnell said at the time, "We never did it before, and we will never do it again. What does a securities analyst know?"[22]

Well, Mr. Bagnell was correct with that comment, but, by and large, what Disney was putting out, with the exception of *TRON* and the movie *Splash* in 1984, the hits were few and far between.

By 1983, Disney had lost $33 million in their film division. They limped along releasing only a handful of movies a year, whereas competing studios were releasing upward of twenty films a year.[23]

In 1984, at the annual stock holders' meeting, under persistent questioning about the situation the studio faced with their films, Ronald Miller, Walt's son-in-law and at the time president and chief executive of Walt Disney Productions, indicated that perhaps the studio would stop making films if they couldn't produce a successful one by 1987.[23]

No more Disney films? Blasphemy! It was really starting to look as though for the first time, Disney was actually in real trouble. Sure, there had always been points in the Disney story, most notably with *Snow White* and again in the creation of Disneyland, when the coffers had been nearly empty and Disney was teetering close to bankruptcy if their gambles didn't pay off. But under Walt and Roy, and by hook or by crook, they had always found a way.

But times were different, and the sharks of the business world were circling the company. In June of 1984, financier Saul Steinberg started buying up enormous chunks of Disney stock. His hopes were to acquire Disney and then dismantle the company for profit, selling off the theme parks and movie library. Steinberg accrued roughly 11 percent of the stock. Not long after, investor Irwin Jacobs tried the same thing with his roughly 7.7 percent stake in Disney stock.[25]

If they couldn't force a take-over, then the name of the game would be "greenmail" (in the vein of the word "blackmail")—buy enough shares, threaten a take-over, and eventually force the company to buy their shares back at a premium.

Which is exactly what happened. Steinberg sold back his shares to Disney for $325 million, a $60 million premium over market value.[24]

Irwin Jacobs had similar success, parlaying his stock greenmail into a $30 million profit.[24]

With Disney investors in an uproar over the corporate raiders feasting on Disney stock and these exorbitant payouts, another Disney family member stepped into the situation.

This family member had Disney blood flowing through his veins (and an enormous stake in the company, at the time roughly 5 percent of the shares). He was the nephew to Walt and son to Roy, Roy E. Disney.[26]

Roy assumed his role as vice chairman of Disney's board of directors (a position he had vacated the year before) and brought with him a few allies, most notably members of the Bass family, who had acquired 25 percent of Disney shares in the battle to stave off Saul Steinberg.[26]

After a tumultuous few months of declining stock prices and two near take-overs, Roy E. Disney was back in the fold. Ronald Miller resigned after eighteen months at the helm of the family business.[24]

In turn, as Miller's replacement, Roy recruited forty-two-year-old Michael Eisner, the president of Paramount Pictures. The dark days at Disney were, hopefully, coming to end. Eisner was an outsider, so to speak. He wasn't a family member or someone who had worked his way up from the mailroom. He was someone who could not only keep pace with the trends of Hollywood but return the studio to the days of setting them.

Eisner would bring a different perspective for tomorrow, without entirely forgetting yesterday. He was a studio executive with a film and television pedigree—something Roy E. Disney valued, as he too had worked in the studio side of things, having grown up in and around the bustling days of Disney.

And as Eisner assumed his role, he was certainly well aware of the valuable treasure trove of entertainment that was dormant in the Disney film vaults. These quotes are from the *New York Times* during Eisner's first week on the job.

> "You could finance a new Disney World by the unused value of our film and television library," he said. "There are 250 episodes of The Wonderful World of Disney and 400 Mickey Mouse cartoons that have never been syndicated. We don't even have a syndication company. Television is an obvious opportunity. For us not to be involved in television is like going to medical school and giving up being a doctor. Any of the series we had at Paramount—'Happy Days,' 'Laverne and Shirley,' 'Taxi'—would have been perfect for Disney.

> "The days when Hanna-Barbera has 90 percent of Saturday morning television will soon be over," he said, referring to the leading producer of children's television programs. "I want to see one Disney show on the air next fall and Disney will now be a competitor in movies with, eventually, a slate of 12 to 15

pictures a year instead of three. Such a bounty has fallen in my lap. Every day a new asset falls out of the sky. The real estate is just the gravy. There are 40 unused acres next to Disneyland planted in strawberries."[27]

But it wasn't only about the movies and television for Eisner. There were plans for the parks as well. Note the last paragraph, with a bit of foreshadowing.

"My six-year-old shouldn't want to go to Knott's Berry Farm," said Mr. Eisner, referring to a park down the road from Disneyland that is crammed with thrill rides. To enliven the Disney parks, whose rides are considered too tame by teen-agers and many younger children, Mr. Eisner is considering expanding Disneyland and Disney World or building parks next door with a separate ticket for entrance.

George Lucas, Steven Spielberg, and Jim Henson, creator of the Muppets, lobbied for Mr. Eisner to get the Disney job. It is not farfetched to guess that Indiana Jones, the Muppets, and the Star Wars pantheon of characters may eventually show up with rides or even worlds of their own at the Disney parks.[27]

It certainly was an interesting time in the Disney story. In many ways the events that took place midway through the decade, made the company so much stronger. Eisner became the catalyst for growth not seen since the day of Walt himself.

We are nearly at the dawn of what many call the Disney Renaissance, but we're not quite there yet. But one thing is for sure: the Michael Eisner era has arrived, and it didn't take long before he made his mark.

In December of 1985, Eisner signed a deal with the French government to bring a Disney Park to France.

In 1986, Disney released their first R-rated movie ever, *Down and Out In Beverly Hills*. It was released under their Touchstone Pictures brand, which was incorporated during the Ron Miller era.[28]

And on the Disneyland front, Eisner tapped a few of his Hollywood connections to create something spectacular for the park. These new attractions brought pop-culture relevance to the theme parks by utilizing story lines that were outside of the Disney catalog.

January 9, 1987

Disney collaborates with George Lucas to bring *Star Tours* to Disneyland.

In 1985, a few guys got together and collaborated on a new project for Disney. Those few guys were Michael Jackson, George Lucas, and Francis Coppola. Their collaboration resulted in the creation of the 3-D sci-fi music film *Captain EO*, which debuted at Disneyland in September of 1986.

Michael Jackson was near the peak of his career, George Lucas was basking in the afterglow of his *Star Wars* franchise, and well, Francis Coppola is Francis Coppola; enough said there.[29]

EO was the perfect recipe for Disney success, featuring some of Hollywood's biggest names to bring something new into the Disney parks. If one attraction featuring George Lucas's creativity was great, then certainly two would be better—especially when that attraction centered on *Star Wars*.

The success of the *Star Wars* franchise was already solidified in the culture of America. Similarly to how Disney became very proficient at adapting their big-screen movies into visually immersive and thrilling attractions at their theme parks, it was time for them to do the same with another film genius's creations—the same genius they had turned down more than a decade ago. But, to be fair, most studios in Hollywood passed on Lucas's *Star Wars*.

Disney committed roughly $32 million to their express trip to Endor. However, this trip would be unlike any other ride at a Disney park, as it took place without really ever physically going anywhere. Instead, guests would have their senses stimulated. Visual displays timed with movements that played upon acceleration, gravity/g-forces, and position tricked the brain into feeling that more intense motions were really taking place.

Imagineers created a groundbreaking theme park attraction with four military flight simulators. George Lucas developed the story line, and Star Tours debuted in 1987, *Star Wars'* tenth anniversary. The attraction was a huge success and revolutionized theme-park attractions. Many theme parks and entertainment centers around the world replicated the concept. Star Tours was already creating lines that were several hours long in Anaheim.[30] Perhaps the same thing could be repeated at a slice of Hollywood Disney was looking to create down in Florida.

January 21, 1988

Disney acquires The Wrather Corporation, finally bringing the Disneyland Hotel under Disney ownership.

Walt Disney knew his oasis in the orange groves, Disneyland, needed a hotel on site to accommodate visitors. Anaheim in 1955 had only eighty-seven hotel rooms collectively. Walt was short on money but deep in dreams.

He turned to his friend, Jack Wrather, to build a hotel adjacent to Disneyland. Wrather, who was a success in his own right in Hollywood with Lassie and the Lone Ranger, eventually agreed and signed a ninety-nine-year lease on the land and built the Disneyland Hotel.

As Disneyland grew and prospered, so did the namesake hotel. Attempts were made several times during Walt's lifetime and after his lifetime to acquire the hotel, but Wrather wasn't selling.

For a brief moment in December of 1972, it appeared that Disney was close to an agreement to bring the hotel into the family of properties, but again, Disney was unsuccessful in the acquisition.[31]

All of that changed sixteen years later, when Disney and an Australian company purchased the Wrather Company. Disney subsequently purchased the Australian firm's interest, leaving them the sole owner of the hotel.[32]

March 29, 1989

The sixty-first Academy Awards were held in Los Angeles, California.

Rain Man, A Fish Called Wanda, Beetlejuice, Who Framed Roger Rabbit, The Accused, Tin Toy, The Accidental Tourist.

Each one of these movies won the coveted Oscar for some aspect of its performance on the big screen. However, only one of these titles holds great significance in the future of Disney, and it's not *Roger Rabbit*.

While *Roger Rabbit* was a highly successful movie for Disney—it made a ton of money, was award winning, and eventually led to a pretty substantial presence at Disneyland—the really significant movie on the list here is *Tin Toy*.

Tin Toy is basically the beginning of commercial success for Pixar. Two weeks after the film won for best animated short, the *New York Times* provided some insight into the film.

For more than a dozen years Alvy Ray Smith and Edwin Catmull, two pioneers in computer graphics, made an annual trek to the Walt Disney Studios to urge that Disney's cartoon animators consider using computers to draw and color the animation frames that have been done by hand since the birth of Mickey Mouse. Each year the Disney people would listen and say, "not yet."

But computer animation is coming of age now. Two weeks ago a cartoon short made entirely by using computer graphics won an Academy Award—a first for the technology—and even Disney has begun to employ it, primarily to fill in the background in scenes.

As a sign of the technology's maturation, those who use it have begun to debate the meaning of the Academy Award. One group says the significant achievement of the cartoon, which tells the story of a windup toy's encounter with a rambunctious baby, is that it illustrates the realism that the technology is capable of achieving. The other group contends that the award is really a recognition of the artistry of the film makers and that computer animation is a powerful tool but one that few have mastered and that cannot realize its full potential without the artist to guide it.

Computer animation is very expensive. The cost of making the award-winning cartoon "The Tin Toy" was several thousand dollars per second of running time, according to its creators. Because of the expense, the technology has been relegated to flying logotypes in television advertisements or brief special-effects work in live-action movies. But the expectation is that costs will come down soon as uses multiply and the necessary computers and software programs become more widespread.

"The Tin Toy" was made by Pixar, a computer graphics company based here. For Mr. Smith, Pixar's executive vice president and co-founder, the Academy Award was affirmation of nearly two decades' work, including writing the first computer "paint" program, in which a mouse is used to draw on a computer.

"We people in computer graphics have known in our bones for 20 years that we would do this," Mr. Smith said of the award. "Our goal is not to have people say, 'That's computer animation'; our goal is photo realism."

Mr. Smith, one of the computer visionaries originally from the Xerox Corporation's Palo Alto Research Center, joined forces about 15 years ago with Mr. Catmull, a professor of computer graphics at the University of Utah. They were originally part of the computer graphics division of Lucasfilm Ltd., and their work appeared in special effects sequences in the "Star Trek" movies II, III and IV; "The Return of the Jedi," and perhaps most dramatically in the stained glass man who came to life in "Young Sherlock Holmes."

The division was spun off as a separate company, Pixar, three years ago and the majority ownership is held by Steven P. Jobs, Apple Computer Inc.'s cofounder, and the founder of Next Inc. Pixar's primary product has been a specialized computer and associated software for very-high-resolution graphics, which is used in medical imaging, scientific visualization and graphic arts design.

Mr. Smith said that long before joining Lucasfilm, he and Mr. Catmull made a pilgrimage every year to Disney to pitch computer technology to the animators, but they were always turned down.

At Disney, however, they met John Lasseter, a traditionally trained animator, whom they later hired at Lucasfilm. The team of Mr. Lasseter with William Reeves and Eben Ostby on the technical side has produced special effects and short films. "The Tin Toy" is their third animated short after "Red's Dream" in 1987 and "Luxo Jr.," which was nominated for a 1986 Academy Award. Mr. Lasseter and Mr. Reeves accepted the Academy Award for "The Tin Toy," thanking among others Mr. Jobs for his support.

This is just a taste of what's to come in the year 1995, when we encounter the film *Toy Story*. But now, it's time for a little taste of Hollywood in central Florida.[33]

May 1, 1989

A third Disney theme park rises in Florida. The Disney-MGM Studios open at Walt Disney World.

Michael Eisner was a busy man during his first five years at the helm of Disney. He made additions and acquisitions, most notably to Disneyland. In 1988, it was time for Eisner to put his stamp on Walt Disney World, a nearly $1 billion stamp.[34] In June of 1988, WDW received the five-star treatment, as in the debut of the lavish waterfront Victorian-style hotel, the Grand Floridian—room rates started at $165 a night in 1988.[35]

If the $165-a-night resort was a bit out of your price range, no worries. In October of 1988, Disney's Caribbean Beach Resort opened with a more moderate room rate. Visit Aruba, Trinidad, Jamaica, Barbados, and Martinique, Disney-style, for $65 a night.[36]

Perhaps you were seeking to experience something a bit more exotic than the Caribbean—say, the beautiful fjords of Norway? Well, that could be arranged, as the Norway Pavilion debuted in the summer of 1988 at EPCOT's World Showcase.[35]

And for those of you looking to spend some time poolside, stateside, Disney debuted the world's largest wave pool at their new water park, Typhoon Lagoon, in June of 1989. An interesting side note: when the plans for the park were announced in 1985, the park was going to be called Splash, after Disney's hit movie from 1984.[37]

Last but not least, in May of 1989, Walt Disney World Village debuted Pleasure Island, an entertainment complex geared toward the night-life-loving older crowd—Pleasure Island survived a few of the name changes at WDW Village, but, by late 2008, it too had succumbed to Disney change.[38]

The building boom at Walt Disney World was underway, but the big story from 1988–1989 was the creation of the Disney-MGM Studios theme park.

The park was announced to the public in 1985.[39] Several factors led to the creation of this park. Michael Eisner knew Disney needed another attraction to extend the average length of stay for guests at the Florida property. And there was another factor at work. Competition was also coming to town.

Despite Sea World setting up shop in 1973, Wet 'n Wild water park in 1977, and Tampa's Busch Gardens about an hour away across Interstate 4, direct competition largely didn't exist for Walt Disney World. That was about to change. Universal Studios announced they were going to build a movie-and-television-based theme park just minutes from Walt Disney World, similar to the park they were operating in Hollywood, California.

Disney heard the industry rumblings about Universal's plans on their turf and sprang into action. On June 27 1985, Disney signed an agreement with MGM/UA Entertainment giving Disney exclusive rights to utilize over 250 of their films in their new park concept. Two weeks later, on July 8, 1985, Michael Eisner officially announced the plans for a third park at Walt Disney World. The park would have an entertainment-based theme, similar to Universal's plan.

If Universal was indeed coming to town, Disney wanted to beat them to the punch. Which is exactly what happened. Disney-MGM Studios opened a full year before Universal Studios. When Universal saw the featured attractions, there were rumblings that Eisner had stolen some of the ideas for Universal's park. In 1981, Eisner was president of Paramount Pictures, and Universal reached out to Paramount to see if the company would have interest in becoming a partner in their park in Florida. They obviously declined, and Eisner eventually joined Disney.[40]

Regardless of whether the idea was stolen or not, the hundred-acre-plus, $300 million park celebrating Hollywood's Golden Age opened its gates on May 1, 1989.

In what has become the norm for a Disney park debut, there was a lot of press coverage, and, of course, the obligatory television special.

When the park debuted, admission was a mere $29 for adults and $23 for children (a four-day passport to visit the other parks as well, for $97 for adults or $77 for children, could be purchased), but the price of admission wasn't just to enjoy a new Disney theme park. It was going to grant you access to an actual working studio complete with sound stages, wardrobes, and everything needed to produce not only animated features but live-action movies and television programs. It was going to be a truly unique endeavor for Disney.

The park's debut was a success. In the month after it opened, Disney stock increased 20 percent. In Disney-MGM's first half year overall, Walt Disney

World attendance grew by five million visits, most by guests extending their stays. The second half of the year saw an increase of another 3.5 million guests.[41]

Despite the success and the millions of guests filling the park, to many visitors, the park had a bit of an identity crisis. Early on guests complained about the size of the park and the lack of attractions. Guests weren't seeing enough of the studio productions. Few people saw live filming on-site, as the name of the park would imply.

As time progressed, little in the way of this improved. Eventually the working studio aspect was abandoned altogether.

Despite little real movie or television production, the park has grown substantially. Some of the most popular attractions in all of Walt Disney World, such as the Tower of Terror, Toy Story Midway Mania, and Aerosmith's Rockin' Roller Coaster, are featured here.

Even with the featured attractions, the identity crisis lingered on until the announcement of major changes hit the news in 2015. Toy Story Land and Star Wars Land were on the Disney drawing board to breathe new life back into the park.

With another Disney park firmly solidifying the company's theme-park presence in America, it was time to give the world something they had been yearning for: an animated Disney film the likes of which the public hadn't seen in decades.

November 15, 1989

Disney's twenty-eighth animated feature, *The Little Mermaid*, is released. The film was a smash hit and won Academy Awards for best score and best song for "Under the Sea."

Welcome to the beginning of the Disney Animation renaissance. *The Little Mermaid* brought Disney out of suspended animation on many levels!

It had been nearly three decades since Disney had animated a fairy tale (the last one had been *Sleeping Beauty* in 1959, and we know from the chapter on the 1950s that it wasn't a success when it debuted) for the big screen.

The Disney rendition of the Hans Christen Andersen fairy tale opened to great fanfare. The *New York Times* gave this glowing review:

"THE LITTLE MERMAID" is a singular treat. This vibrant, bright, tuneful, beautifully animated children's film is much too quick and savvy to appeal solely to children. Its dry humor, its saucy modern heroine and its terrific score are enchanting for viewers of every age. This ranks with the very best of Disney's animated films—certainly it's the best new one in 30 years—and it's an unqualified delight.

In just 24 days in fewer than 1,000 theaters, "The Little Mermaid" has sold more than $26 million worth of tickets, and Christmas vacation—the prime season for the movie—has not even begun."[42]

In 2011, *Time* magazine named it one of the 25 All-TIME Best Animated Films. Ahh, animated Disney success, welcome back, old friend! The movie was not only a critical but a commercial success. With a budget of around $40 million, the eventual box office returns brought in a fivefold return of roughly $200 million from a worldwide release—not to mention merchandise and live stage shows. Disney was back and thirsty for more animated success.

It seems as though Disney was hitting their stride after just a few years with Michael Eisner in control. Success was on both sides of the Disney coin—theme park and screen success. The 1980s could be called the decade of Michael Eisner. He breathed new life into the company. According to Eisner, these five years were just the beginning, as an all-out Disney invasion was about to take over—or, as he proclaimed it, the nineties were to be the Decade of Disney.

CHAPTER SEVEN

1990S

As we saw, the seventies and eighties were great decades for the Disney theme park lover but were mostly disappointing for enthusiasts of Disney's animated fairy tales. All of that changed in the 1990s, as the studio pumped out some of their most beloved hits during this decade.

The Walt Disney Company (the name was officially changed from Walt Disney Productions to the Walt Disney Company in February 1986), most notably their studio division, endured a shift in culture from a struggle to prosperity during this decade.

Reminiscent of the days when Walt was in charge, the catalyst was the animated feature film. The studio homed in on the public's love for Disney big-screen animation.

The releases of *Beauty and the Beast*, *Aladdin*, and *The Lion King*, along with *Toy Story*, propelled the studio to new heights.

However, the limelight wasn't exclusive to movies; the theme parks would star in a production Michael Eisner dubbed "The Decade of Disney."

In January of 1990, Michael Eisner announced his incredibly ambitious plan: "In the next decade, we will do nothing less than reinvent the Disney wheel."[1]

> "A fourth theme park, a Soviet pavilion, and seven new hotels will be among major projects to be built during a decade of rapid expansion at Florida's Disney World," company chairman Michael Eisner announced Sunday.
>
> The 1990s will also feature the entertainment conglomerate's venture into time-share vacation units, and it will open 29 new attractions at its three existing parks—the Magic Kingdom, Epcot Center and the Disney-MGM Studios.

The Walt Disney Co. will open Euro Disneyland near Paris and build studio attractions at its Japanese and California parks during the next few years among other additions, Eisner said.

"But the parks are the place where the 'Disney Decade' will have the most impact," he said.

The company's objectives are to grow about 20 percent a year "and have a return on equity of 20 percent for the next decade...so we can stay healthy."

Disney expects total attendance at all its parks to approach 100 million visits a year by the end of the century. The company anticipates a strong national economy over the decade but that some of Disney's plans could be modified if there is a drastic downturn.

Otherwise, he said, "Everything we have announced will definitely be built...When we announce something, it happens."[2]

Disney officials would not give any details on the fourth park or say when construction would begin. Negotiations with Soviet officials have been taking place for years, and an agreement on a Soviet pavilion at Epcot Center is near, Eisner said. Also to be announced soon are plans for a Swiss pavilion featuring a Matterhorn ride.

Most of the focus at the start of the decade will be on new hotels and expanding the newest central Florida park, Disney-MGM Studios, because "its overwhelming success caught us off guard," the Disney chief said.

Sixteen new shows will double the capacity of the attractions and exhibits in the next five years.

Seven new or remodeled attractions will be introduced at the Magic Kingdom and five at Epcot Center, he said.[3]

Wow, those were some bold plans. And how about that quote, "When we announce something, it happens."

So what happened to the Soviet and Swiss pavilions? Well, on the Soviet front, rumors are the FBI was a bit apprehensive about the possibility of foreign nationals from communist countries working at the World Showcase.

Through the Freedom of Information Act, hundreds of FBI pages were released in late 2015 via the organization MuckRock. The files detailed the bureau's interest in EPCOT, most notably the Chinese pavilion. The documents are posted on thedisneystory.com.[4]

FBI or no FBI, the Soviet Union collapsed in late 1991. Obviously, a presence at WDW wasn't a priority for the country at that point.

So, if the shady premise of Russian spies masquerading around with Mickey Mouse never came to be under the decade of Disney, how about another un-Disney-like activity, such as gambling, and then fast food? These two topics were also floated out to the public in the early 1990s, with one of the concepts coming to fruition.

April 5, 1991

Disney announces plans for a nationwide lottery program.

Lookout, Powerball. Here comes Mickeyball! In April of 1991, Disney's Buena Vista Television unit announced plans to syndicate a half-hour lottery show for the fall of 1992.

The program planned to have a game-show format for thirty-three state lotteries. The state lotteries would combine their lottery money into a single cash pool that would allow for prizes into the millions of dollars.

Television viewers in participating lottery states would be able to take part directly in the game. Residents of nonlottery states wouldn't be able to play but might be involved in tie-in promotions sponsored by local stores.

Game pieces would have been available for purchase at that state's lottery agents for each night's game.

> Randy Reiss, then executive vice president of Walt Disney Studios, remarked, "It is unlikely that Disney characters would be part of the show." Disney does not view its involvement with a lottery as counter to the company's family-oriented image.

"We decided that lotteries in those states are voted on…These are the state's decision, and we are the last company in the world that would fall into any kind of censorship. We are not issuing judgment on such games."[5]

Fast-forward two months later. On June 4, 1991, Disney announced the cancellation of their lottery show, commenting that their involvement might be perceived as encouraging children to gamble.[6]

Another unlikely venue Disney dabbled in during the early 1990s was a fast-food enterprise. A few years earlier, in March of 1987, Disney opened their first retail store outside of a Disney park, at the Glendale Galleria in California.

Perhaps it was only natural that they would double down on their mall presence and try to capitalize on feeding the masses.

On April 28, 1990, Disney opened their fiftieth retail Disney store, at the Montclair Plaza Mall, roughly thirty-five miles east of Los Angeles. Adjacent to the location was Mickey's Kitchen.[7]

A year later, a second Mickey's Kitchen debuted, in Schaumburg, Illinois, about forty miles northwest of Chicago.

The two restaurants featured items such as Goofy's Burger, Supercalifragi-Chickensalad, Salads-in-Wonderland, Piglet Corkscrew Fries, and, of course, everyone's favorite, "Soup-a-dee-doo-dah."[8]

Mickey's Kitchen didn't last very long. By March of 1992, Disney had closed the kitchen doors, citing a lackluster performance and saying that the concept had merely been an experiment.

Disney was probably ahead of their time with this concept, as the restaurant featured a wide variety of healthy, lower-calorie, low-fat items, such as meatless burgers, turkey hot dogs, and fresh fruit shakes.[9] With the healthy food initiatives Disney has embraced over the past few years within their theme parks and their branded foods in grocery stores, perhaps it's time for Disney revisit Mickey's Kitchen!

November 22, 1991

Beauty and the Beast is released. It's the first animated feature to receive a nomination for the Academy Award for best picture.

A tale as old as time—or at least really, really, ancient. Researchers in 2016 announced the fairy tale known loosely as *Beauty and the Beast* dates back four thousand years.[10]

We are all aware the overall story: a hideous creature and a beautiful woman fall in love. The tale has been recounted many times and via many entertainment genres.

Disney got in on the action in November of 1991 with their award-winning animated feature film, followed it up with a Broadway show in 1994, and even put the show on ice in the late 1990s when Walt Disney World on Ice toured the country.

Disney spent roughly $14 million sending *Beast* to Broadway in April of 1994. This figure made the production the most expensive one in history. In reality, $14 million was a paltry number considering the film grossed over $350 worldwide during its first three years, but nonetheless, the $14 million was well spent, as the Broadway show was nominated for several Tony Awards and played on Broadway for over a decade.[11]

But when it came to awards and recognition, Disney's *Beauty and the Beast* captivated the entertainment world when it was nominated for Oscar's Best Picture at the sixty-fourth Academy Award nominations—a first for a full-length animated feature film..[12]

Unfortunately, the film didn't take home the hardware for Best Picture (it won for best song and best score), and, around nomination time, there was an interesting blurb as to why animated films don't usually even warrant best-picture nominations.

> There are several theories why animation gets the short shaft. One holds that the Academy voters—whose largest branch is 1,336 living, breathing, three-dimensional actors—don't like voting for two-dimensional drawings.
>
> Another maintains that animated movies of the last several years—such as "Robin Hood," "The Aristocats," "The Black Cauldron," and "All Dogs Go to Heaven"—were so inept the whole genre was relegated to the backwaters of Hollywood.
>
> Then there's the Academy bias for the "serious" movies.[13]

There you have it: Disney's *Black Cauldron* strikes again! Obviously, it was an honor that *Beauty and the Beast* was even nominated in the category. Despite losing the Academy Award, the film has become an all-time Disney classic. Since 2012, the film's popularity can still be felt at Walt Disney World. With the expansion of Fantasyland, the movie now features prominently, with the Be Our Guest Restaurant, Gaston's Tavern, and a replica of Beast's castle.

April 12, 1992

Euro Disney, Disney's first theme park in Europe, located twenty miles east of Paris, France, opens.

Euro Disney—renamed Disneyland Paris in 1994—oh boy, where to start with this topic. This park is one of the first "bumps in the road" during the Michael Eisner campaign.

Even before Eisner joined the company, Disney was entertaining the notion of a park in Europe. In February of 1984, then president Ronald Miller told the *New York Times* the company was in negotiations with several European countries. Most notable were Britain and West Germany.[14]

In March of 1987, Eisner made the announcement, and the agreements were signed. Disney was coming to France.

From Disney's perspective, expectations and optimism were high, and so was their case of cultural imperialism, according to the French. Here is a sampling from the *New York Times* about a year before the park debuted.

> With great fanfare, three $150 million amusement parks opened in France in the past three years, but all have fallen flat, and two have been forced into bankruptcy.
>
> Nonetheless, the Walt Disney Company is pushing hard with plans to open Europe's first Disneyland next year, a $4.4 billion extravaganza sprawling over 5,000 acres of former sugar beet fields 20 miles east of Paris.
>
> No one at the company is even having second thoughts. Disney being Disney, executives instead are worried that Euro Disneyland—covering an area one-fifth the size of Paris itself—just might not be big enough to handle the crowds. In a move that would border on hubris at almost any other

company, plans are already being drawn for emergency radio and subway announcements to warn people away when the park fills up.

"My biggest fear," said Robert Fitzpatrick, Euro Disneyland's chairman, "is that we will be too successful."

"I don't think it can miss," said Margo Vignola, an analyst with Salomon Brothers. "They are masters of marketing. When the place opens, it will be perfect. And they know how to make people smile—even the French."

To be sure, not everyone is glad that Mickey & Company are coming to the Continent. When Disney's chairman, Michael Eisner, visited Paris's Bourse to launch Euro Disney's stock offering, leftist demonstrators greeted him with eggs, globs of ketchup and "Mickey Go Home" signs. And some French intellectuals have complained that Disney characters will pollute the nation's cultural ambiance; one dubbed Euro Disneyland "a cultural Chernobyl." Indeed, in negotiating with Disney, French officials dropped heavy hints that they would like a little less American kitsch and a little more European culture at France's Magic Kingdom.

Euro Disneyland will come complete with a golf course, a Davy Crockett campground, an ice-skating rink inspired by Rockefeller Centers and six Disney-owned hotels with 5,200 rooms. But Disney's ambitions do not stop there. The company is planning a $3 billion second phase, with a Disney MGM studio and visitors' tour to open in 1994 as well as 13,000 more hotel rooms. It is also weighing a European Epcot.

"There is tremendous future growth for our company in Europe," Mr. Eisner said in a telephone interview.

One of the reasons Mr. Eisner is so confident is that Europeans love Disney's American parks: they accounted for 2.7 million visits last year. And they love the Mickey magazines and T-shirts, Little Mermaid records and other Disney paraphernalia, so much that they spent $1.6 billion on Disney merchandise last year.

Mr. Eisner is so keen on Europe that Disney has taken a 49 percent stake in the Euro Disney project, the maximum the French Government will allow.

Once the park opens, the real payoff begins. The company will receive 10 percent of Euro Disney's admission fees and 5 percent of food and merchandise revenues, the same arrangement as in Japan. But in France, it will also receive management fees, incentive fees and 49 percent of the profits.

What makes the European numbers even sweeter is that Disney has put up only $160 million for the project. Other investors have pumped in $1.2 billion in equity; the French Government has provided a low-interest $960 million loan and banks have lent another $1.6 billion. The rest—some $400 million—comes from special partnerships formed to buy properties and lease them back.

Euro Disneyland will be similar to its American counterparts. Disney's "imagineers" have not forgotten to add some French accents—and some British, Italian and German ones as well. The park will have two official languages, English and French, and multilingual guides on hand to help Dutch, German, Spanish and Italian visitors.

"Europe isn't North America," said Mr. Fitzpatrick, whose office is dominated by a seven-foot-tall Mickey Mouse tapestry. "It seemed appropriate and politically astute to underline that Pinocchio was an Italian boy, Peter Pan used to fly out of London and Cinderella was a French girl. We've tried to re-emphasize the European roots of these stories."

Still, the new Disneyland will remain far more American than European. "It would have been silly to take Mickey Mouse and try to do surgery to create a transmogrified hybrid, half French and half American," Mr. Fitzpatrick said.

And Disney has had the audacity to banish wine (and other alcoholic beverages) from France's Magic Kingdom, just as in its other parks.

"To the untrained eye, this Magic Kingdom will be very similar to Tokyo Disneyland and the Magic Kingdom in Florida," said Mr. Eisner.

Can the mix of American and European influences attract—and hold—an audience? No question, says Mr. Fitzpatrick, who adds that his real concern is that too many people will come at peak times, forcing Euro Disney to shut its gates after its 50,000-person capacity is reached.[15]

Before Euro Disney opened, the park's success could be analogous with a coin toss, whether Disney knew it or not. One side was what Disney thought the folks of Europe wanted, and the other was the reality of what Parisians and Europeans wanted. Basing the park in Paris on the great success Disney had received in Japan, the company chose the wrong side of the coin flip.

Disney was steadfast and strong minded—or naïve, depending how you view it—about what their European park should be. Indeed, the decades of building parks lent to this confidence, in addition to the demographics of the millions of Europeans who were making the trek to see the mouse stateside.

But, as we know, and as Disney had to know, every culture is different. But the writing was on the wall early; Disney was going to do things their way—note that a year before the park was even open, they had already decided no wine or alcohol for the park. *Sacre bleu*!

The quote of "cultural Chernobyl" or the "Mickey Go Home" greeting Michael Eisner received apparently didn't resonate with the company either. The list of snafus and misguided quotes from Disney could go on and on—countless articles and entire books have been devoted to this topic. The subject turned into a case study of what not to do when looking to expand your business internationally.

Well, Disney pressed on, and the park opened in spectacular fashion. Like each of the parks before it, Euro Disney was the setting for a spectacular grand opening, ripe with celebrities who jetted to France to put on a good show for the mouse. The event was broadcast live to France, Britain, Italy, Germany, and Spain and shown in the States on a delay.[16]

After the festivities were over, it was all downhill from there. The problems with the park were plenty. There were issues and grievances filed with unions regarding noncompliant park employees snubbing their noses at the Disney-required grooming habits and dress codes.

Many farmers who were displaced when Disney and the government commandeered their land were protesting the park. Perhaps worst of all were the comments throughout the media that Disney was an assault on the French culture, that Disney just "didn't get it."

By the end of its first year of operation, the park had lost over $900 million, a loss of nearly $2.5 million a day. At one point in late 1993, Eisner confirmed that closing the park down was a possibility.

> "If the engine of an airplane falls out in full flight, what are the options? Anything is possible today, including the closure of Euro Disney," Michael Eisner was quoted.
>
> Disney holds 49 percent of Euro Disney and is preparing to wrangle with 60 creditor banks over the restructuring and refinancing of the 18-month-old theme park near Paris.
>
> He called the theme park the first real financial disappointment since he took over the company in September 1984. "This has been a very serious problem," Eisner told shareholders.[18]

As time revealed, the park never closed. However, it still hemorrhaged money for years. Finally, in late 1995, for the first time, the park reported an annual profit.[19]

By 2014, financial trouble was looming for the park again. Despite drawing upward of fourteen million visitors (the park outdraws the Louvre, the world's most-visited museum, also located in France), the park was teetering again on financial insolvency. Disney announced they were committing $1.2 billion to the park to provide some stability.

November 11, 1992

Disney's thirty-first animated feature, *Aladdin*, is released.

> Any doubts that the studio could return to the glory days of "Snow White" and "Fantasia" were blown away by last year's stunning commercial and critical success of "Beauty and the Beast," which, in addition to becoming the first animated film

ever to earn an Academy Award best picture nomination, took in more than $140 million.

"We *hate* talking about this," Katzenberg says in an interview, "because I'm convinced that if we ever allow the business of these movies to take center stage, it will corrupt the pureness of what takes place (in the animation department). As soon as we start worrying about whether the next movie will make more than the last one, then I believe that's the beginning of the end."[22]

The above quote is from Jeffrey Katzenberger, who at the time was chairman of Disney Studios. It sounds like something Walt Disney would have said. If you recall, he said something similar to this after the success of *Mary Poppins*.

Aladdin was released less than six months after *Beauty and the Beast*. That is certainly a tough show to follow, but in the end, *Aladdin* held its own.

Beast cast a large shadow over *Aladdin*, but as anyone who has watched the movie knows, *Aladdin* featured an enormous personality, a character who stole the show and allowed the film to separate itself from previous Disney animated movies.

Love him or hate him, the late great Robin Williams was often larger than life; this can be seen in his role as the Genie—a role he asked Disney not to advertise.

"We always thought of Robin Williams as the Genie," Clements says. "And we wrote him that way from the start.

"There was a line in one of the bits, where Robin says to the audience, 'Tonight, I want to talk to you about the very serious problem of schizophrenia.' In the animation, I had him grow another head, so he could argue with himself about it."

Williams found himself in a recording booth at George Lucas' Skywalker recording studios in Marin County, armed only with a microphone and a script and the assurances from Clement and Musker that was he free to improvise as much as he wanted.

"We never thought that Robin would come in and just read the script as we'd written it," Musker says. "And he didn't."

What they got, in that initial four-hour recording session, was their first real indication of just how different "Aladdin" could be. Although they had written the script with Williams's free-form shtick in mind, they hadn't expected that he would careen into such a dizzying barrage of characters. One minute he was an evangelist screaming "Yay-esss! Hallelujah!" and the next he was Walter Cronkite. The first scene alone he tackled 25 times, in 25 different ways, stretching and bending premises to the point that scenes originally meant to last 30 seconds suddenly were 10 minutes long.

"Come on down. Look at this," Williams would say at one point, pretending to be a fast-talking merchant in a Middle Eastern bazaar. "Combination hookah and coffee maker. And it also makes julienne fries.

"And this? I have never seen one of these intact before. The famous Dead Sea Tupperware. Ahhh. Still good."

"Believe me, Robin Williams is more than a performer in this movie, he is a co-author," says Katzenberg, claiming not to be bothered by the fact that Williams declined to have his name mentioned in any of "Aladdin's" marketing materials, not even the production notes for the press, in which the name of every other performer (including comedian Gilbert Gottfried as a nasty parrot named Iago) is listed.

"We didn't hire him for his celebrity or his marquee value," Katzenberg says, pointing out that Williams has every right to reserve his promotional energies for another film, Barry Levinson's "Toys," coming out next month. "We hired him for his talent."[22]

November 11, 1993

Disney announces their plans for a new theme park located in Prince William County, Virginia, just outside of Washington DC, Disney's America.

Every few years, a Disney theme park rumor floats around. Surely you've heard them: Disney is coming here, there, and everywhere. As recently as 2015, a man was convicted and sentenced to over seventeen years in prison for running a fraudulent investment scheme in which he convinced over 280 investors to invest over $20 million in land deals that were going to be on the fringes of the new theme park Disney was building in North Texas.

After Disney announced the park, investors would flip the land for a profit once property values skyrocketed.[23]

One small problem: there was no theme park in the works—Disney executives even testified during the case and commented that North Texas would never be an option, as it could hurt attendance at both Disneyland and WDW.[24]

OK, so there was no shot Disney was going to build a park in Texas. Wait a minute. Actually, for a brief time in 1985, Disney collaborated with the developer Rouse and tentatively planned for an urban entertainment shopping complex called Texposition in Dallas, but this concept was discarded by 1988.[25] But what about a park in Virginia?

Yes, this almost came to be. As the story goes, in 1991, Michael Eisner visited Williamsburg, Virginia, and said he was convinced "that a park based on historical and patriotic themes could succeed, if we found the right place for it."[26]

By 1993, Disney found a place outside of Washington, DC, in Prince William County, in the community of Haymarket. As the company had done previously, they tried to acquire the land, roughly three thousand acres, quietly.

On November 8, 1993, the *Wall Street Journal* leaked a story that Disney was looking to do battle with the Paramount Studios–owned theme park Kings Dominion near Richmond, Virginia.

The details about the park were still sketchy, but Disney did acquire land somewhere in Virginia, and a working title of the park was Walt Disney's America.[27]

Three days later, Michael Eisner officially announced the park, and here's what he described:

> The American history theme park that Walt Disney Co. plans
> to build west of Washington will include, "painful, disturbing

and agonizing" exhibits on slavery, American Indian life, and the Vietnam War, unlike the fantasy attractions at the company's other parks, Disney Chairman Michael D. Eisner said yesterday.

"We are going to be sensitive, but we will not be showing the absolute propaganda of the country," Eisner said.

Disney officials said that like the company's other parks, the one to be built in Prince William County will celebrate all that is American. But by showing the not-so-sunny side of the American experience, the company that brought Mickey Mouse and Donald Duck to life plans to show a bit of an edge in its new park.

"This is not a Pollyanna view of America," said Bob Weis, a Disney senior vice president.

"We want to make you a Civil War soldier. We want to make you feel what it was like to be a slave or what it was like to escape through the underground railroad," Weis told a packed room of reporters, local and state politicians and community residents. He described in detail the nine different historical theme areas of the park.

Peter Rummell, president of Disney Design and Development, said the company isn't concerned that the park's attractions will violate standards of political correctness. "An intelligent story properly told shouldn't offend anybody," he said.

The park also would have thrill rides, including a wooden roller coaster and a 60-foot Ferris wheel. In an area of the park devoted to the Industrial Revolution, tourists would visit a simulated factory town and take a high-speed ride through a turn-of-the-century mill, simulating an escape from a fiery vat of molten steel.

The plan outlined yesterday by Disney officials was revealed after more than two years in which undercover Disney representatives secretly bought or obtained options on land in Prince William County. They used false names and kept

Disney's interest in the area secret to prevent land prices from soaring.

The park, which Disney officials said would have an entrance with a Civil War motif and be closed only about six weeks during January and February, would open by the spring of 1998 and create 3,000 permanent jobs, Rummell said. About 2,000 people would be hired to build the park, he said.

The plan, which sources said could attract an estimated 30,000 visitors a day during peak periods, drew wide praise at yesterday's news conference from state and local officials, most of whom learned of the project only recently.

The park would be near increasingly congested Interstate 66, and would require hundreds of millions of dollars in road and other transportation improvements. Because the project would bring thousands of cars to the area, it would need an endorsement from a regional panel that is struggling to find ways to clean the Washington area's air, which exceeds federal standards for pollution.

And the Disney project is likely to face opposition from a feisty anti-growth movement in western Prince William, which crushed a developer's plans five years ago to build a shopping mall adjacent to the Manassas Battlefield.

Neither Disney nor state officials offered specifics yesterday about how much state and local money might be required for public improvements. But Virginia Gov. L. Douglas Wilder and Gov.-elect George F. Allen said they believe it makes sense for taxpayers to bear part of the bill because of the state and local tax revenue that would be produced by the Disney project, which company officials estimate would be $1.5 billion over 30 years.

"I think it'll be a moneymaker for the state," said Allen, who learned of the project recently while visiting Walt Disney World in Florida. "Our administration will certainly kick down any hurdles."

Other officials expressed reservations about what they saw as a lack of details about how the project would be financed.

Disney officials said the 100-acre park and a 27-hole public golf course would be built in the project's first phase.

Disney officials say they will submit their proposal by the end of the month to Prince William officials, who already have promised to quickly consider it. The county will aim for July 1994 approval, which would allow Disney to meet its goal of beginning construction in 1995. Getting zoning approval for such a project normally takes about two years.

Eventually, the company plans some residential and commercial development as a buffer between the park and neighboring properties. Officials said that Disney isn't planning to build a major shopping center, but might put in some retail shops.[28]

The new enterprise in Virginia was starting to sound like the blueprint for Walt Disney World. Covert land deals via dummy corporations—check. Concessions and a possible sweet deal from the state legislature—check. Throw in the prospect of residential housing—check.

Well, that's where the comparisons to WDW come to an end, because this theme park didn't move much further than the Disney drawing boards and instead went into the discarded Disney file.

Briefly, here's what went down. The land Disney purchased was not too far from some hallowed grounds—actual real American history, the Civil War battlefields at Manassas. Historians and locals around the area were not happy with the prospect of a Disney park in their area, and they waged a battle of their own to stop Disney.

Groups started to come together to halt the project. One group, Protect Historic America, pointed out that the park would be between the hills and farmland of Washington and the Blue Ridge Mountains. Disney's site was situated within an hour's drive of thirteen historic towns, sixteen Civil War battle sites, and seventeen historic districts. If Disney came to town, these areas would be overwhelmed with traffic and would see a "commercial blitzkrieg" of motels, gas stations, and shops, and the group used photographs of what had popped up around Disneyland to drive home their point.[29]

Wow. A brilliant example from the group. As we know, Walt purchased large quantities of land in Florida so he could avoid the repeat of the commercialization he saw pop up around Disneyland.

If this perspective didn't sway Disney, then here come a few academics to join the conversation. Here's a blurb from the *Washington Post*, from May of 1994:

> A group of prominent American historians and writers has formed to oppose the Walt Disney Co.'s planned theme park in Northern Virginia, criticizing what one of them called the park's potential for the "commercialization and vulgarization" of the nation's past. The group, led by Yale University professor emeritus C. Vann Woodward and Duke University scholar John Hope Franklin, has about 20 members and includes biographer and essayist Arthur Schlesinger Jr.; historians James McPherson, Barbara Fields, Doris Kearns Goodwin, Shelby Foote and David McCullough; novelist William Styron; journalist Tom Wicker; and Richard Moe, head of the National Trust for Historic Preservation.
>
> Building Disney's America 35 miles west of Washington "would be an appalling commercialization and vulgarization of the scene of our most tragic history, and I would deplore it," said Woodward, author of "Origins of the New South" and a dean of Southern history.
>
> Many historians have said the park's construction near Haymarket would amount to putting a small city on farmland surrounded by more than two dozen sites from the Revolutionary and Civil wars.[30]

And with that, say good-bye to Disney's America. The opposition from preservationists and historians, along with a great deal of bad publicity for Disney, killed the project a mere thirteen months after it was announced. Many were shocked that Disney pulled the plug that quickly.

What probably isn't shocking is the notion that the state was truly behind the project and was working to fast-track it. As the governor proclaimed in the first few days of the project, "I think it'll be a moneymaker for the state; our administration will certainly kick down any hurdles."

In January of 1994, Governor Allen presented his package of incentives for Disney to the Virginia General Assembly, and two months later, in March, they approved a $160 million dollar package for Disney.

On September 21, 1994, a local planning board voted 7–1 for zoning changes requested by Disney and recommended the Board of Supervisors approve the project.

A week later, on September 28, Disney announced they would abandon the site.[31] The opposition to the park became too much. As Michael Eisner commented, "There was no project during my first decade at Disney about which I felt more passionate than Disney's America—and none that ran up against fiercer resistance."[26]

Well, the public got their way. And truth be told, who knows what actually would have come to fruition. We've seen the plans change many times from Disney over the years.

As good as Disney is, even with all the pixie dust in the world, slavery and the multitude of wars this country waged are delicate subjects to deal in, especially within the setting of a theme park.

And in the end, part of what Disney wanted to bring to these tracts of land in Virginia did come to fruition—there is a slew of residential homes.

June 15, 1994

The Lion King premieres in New York and Los Angeles. The film opens nationwide on June 24, 1994.

Hakuna matata is a phrase in Swahili that loosely translates into English as "no worries"—which is something Disney had when they released *The Lion King* in the summer of 1994.

The film was practically a Disney classic overnight. The studio handpicked an all-star celebrity cast to voice the characters in the movie, which was inspired by Shakespeare's *Hamlet*.[32]

James Earl Jones, Jeremy Irons, Matthew Broderick, Whoopi Goldberg (no relation to the author!), Jonathan Taylor Thomas, and Cheech Marin, to name a few.

Combine these voices with the creativity of roughly six hundred of Disney's artists and animators, merchandise the heck out of the film, and what you have is an enormous financial success for Disney.[32]

A year after the film's release, *The Lion King* grossed roughly $313 million, along with over $1 billion from total merchandise sales.[33]

Disney licensed more than a thousand products associated with the movie.[34] Mattel, who produced countless toys for the film, couldn't produce items fast enough for consumer demand. Burger King, who held exclusive rights to market the movie in the fast-food sector, exhausted their supply of thirty million toys for kids' meals in under seven weeks, having given away seventeen million within the first two weeks.[35]

Even the east African nation of Uganda hopped on the film's gravy train and released a set of twenty-seven different *Lion King* postage stamps.[35]

The film crushed the box office; it even brought Disney their first number-one album since *Mary Poppins*.

All of this success led to more merchandising opportunities, a Broadway show and then a national touring show, a few video and DVD releases; the list could go on.

The Lion King brought us waist deep into the renaissance of Disney animation. Another jewel was added to the Disney crown with this movie. Disney was truly the king of the medium again. It was a remarkable five years in the studio: 1989's *The Little Mermaid*, 1991's *Beauty and the Beast*, 1992's *Aladdin*, and 1994's *The Lion King*.

The studio had great scripts, and it made incredible decisions with casting. And, of course, the animators and artists were marvelous. Those working in the studio seemed to be channeling their inner Walt. They strived for better production after each picture and began incorporating new technology into each film. Here are a few lines from Tony Bancroft, an animator on the movie.

> The pressure on animators to continually best themselves increases with each release. "This is the new golden era of animation for Disney" says Bancroft, the animation supervisor.

Just don't assume the indelible images are the result of some newfangled technological marvel. Though it's tempting to credit the studio's ever-improving animated output to cutting-edge hardware, the actual explanation is a lot earthier: the "practice makes perfect" adage.

"Any artist will tell you that if you're not continually striving to improve, you're dying as an artist. I think all of us strive to do better and better with every film we make. Twenty percent of improvements you see on the screen are due to technology, and 80% are due to experience—and the desire to do better," says Bancroft.

Advancements in computer animation techniques did allow "The Lion King" artists to mount more ambitious sequences than ever before, like the two-minute stampede of thousands of wildebeests.

But as Bancroft adds, "That technology is still very minimal to us. It...has a very small function in these films."

Thus, the bulk of "The Lion King" was done the old fashioned way: 119,058 individually colored frames of film, set against 1,197 hand-painted backgrounds.[32]

But all of that would soon change. A year and a half after "The Lion King" debuted, a film was released that would leave an indelible mark not only on the animated film industry but on Disney itself.

Sit tight, because we aren't there just yet. There's one more story to read, something more along the lines of a Disney human-interest story.

June 10, 1994

Thelma Pearl Howard dies just days before her eightieth birthday.

OK, so I'm sure you're wondering who Thelma Howard was. She was Walt Disney's live-in housekeeper and cook beginning in 1951. Thelma, or Fou Fou, as she was affectionately called by those around her, was the Disney family's real-life Mary Poppins for roughly thirty years—that is, if Poppins were a chain smoker and a bit rough around the edges, but very much a loving person.

So why did Thelma make it into *The Disney Story*? you ask. Well, it appears that Thelma was a fairy godmother in her own right. Here's a blurb from the Associated Press after she passed away:

> Starting back in the 1950s, she was given a few shares of stock for Christmas and birthdays and that sort of thing. She was told to hang onto it, and she did. She never sold a share of it. I don't think she knew what it was worth. She had great faith in the Disneys and wouldn't part with it.[37]

As the quote reveals, Walt gave Thelma some shares of Disney stock during her stint as his housekeeper. Thelma held onto her Disney stock for more than four decades. With the ebb and flow of stock prices over the decades, it turned out the shares Walt had given her were worth quite a bit of money—millions, in fact.

When Thelma passed away, she left an estate worth around $9 million. Half of the estate went to her only child, Michael, who was living in a home for the developmentally disabled. The other half of her estate was left to charities that helped poor and disabled children. Now there's a story even the Disney studio couldn't write!

November 22, 1995

Toy Story, the first full-length animated feature created entirely by computer, is released.

Let's revisit the previous chapter for a moment. In 1989, an upstart computer company, Pixar, produced an animated short that won an Academy Award.

As their story goes, Pixar repeatedly tried to sell Disney their technology, to no avail. But obviously, an Academy Award couldn't be ignored.

In 1991, Pixar signed a production agreement with Disney; Pixar was obligated to deliver at least three full-length, computer-animated feature films. Which brings us to *Toy Story*.[38]

The release of this film wasn't as succinct as it sounds in the lines above. The four years from the time Disney and Pixar came together to create the movie was anything but easy for the Pixar crew.

As John Lasseter often recounts, the project was rife with issues. A couple of actors named Bill both passed voicing Buzz Lightyear (Billy Crystal and Bill Murray; at one point, even Jim Carey was in the mix).[39]

However, securing their desired voice talent was hardly Pixar's biggest issue. Almost two years to the day before the film debuted, the plug was nearly pulled on Woody and the gang.

On November 19, 1993, the team working on the film went to meet with their bosses at Disney to present a collection of filmed storyboards illustrating their vision for the movie. Disney hated what they saw.

At the time, Disney animation chief Peter Schneider told them, "Guys, no matter how much you try to fix it, it just isn't working."

Not only was the film not musical, something Disney wanted, but it wasn't funny or endearing. The chemistry between Woody and Buzz didn't seem right, and, as John Lasseter remarked, "Woody was a jerk."[41]

Fearing Disney was going to terminate their deal, John Lasseter, Peter Docter, and Andrew Stanton regrouped back at their studio.

The trio knew what they wanted for their movie. They wanted it to stand on its own, separate from what Disney had created with the music-centric *Beauty and the Beast* and *Aladdin*.[42]

> "We kind of made a list of what we didn't want our movie to be," Lasseter said. "We didn't want a break-out-in-song musical. We didn't want it to be fairy-tale. We had done a short film, "Tin Toy," and felt the idea of toys coming alive when people weren't around had a lot of possibilities.
>
> "We felt the key was the choosing of the toys," said Lasseter. "We did a lot of research into the types of toys that were around when we were kids."
>
> They realized there had been no animated buddy pictures. The genre, Lasseter said, "satisfied our desire to have the main characters be the most interesting characters. We were interested in having flawed main characters. There is a tendency to have the villain or the secondary characters be the most interesting characters. They are afraid to make the leads flawed."

They also decided to make the toys adults. "They are not children themselves, so when the toys come alive, we kind of made it more like a workplace," Lasseter said. "We started populating the film with contrasting types of characters, and we found ourselves putting ourselves into all of these characters."[42]

The group grabbed some Pixar dust (it's the computer version of Pixie dust) sprinkled some on the story, and poof, the story line of Andy and his toy-mangling neighbor came to be. The reworked story was a success, Disney was back onboard, and, as the saying goes, the rest is history.

Toy Story went on to become the top-grossing film of the year and was nominated for countless awards. But perhaps nothing speaks more to the movie's legacy than this fact. Since the release of *Toy Story*, there have been more than 250 computer-animated features released.[42]

As for John Lasseter, much in the way the film redefined animation, his influence over the medium also followed the same trajectory. We will see much more of John over the next chapter.

January 4, 1996

Stockholders approve Disney's merger with Capital Cities/ABC.

On July 31, 1995, things came full circle for the Walt Disney Company. The very company that had helped launch them into the theme park business was now a disciple in their kingdom. Disney announced they were acquiring the American Broadcasting Company (ABC) for $19 billion.

The deal had almost happened two years earlier, but Eisner reportedly balked at the price, which at the time was $11 billion.[43]

When Disney finally pulled the trigger on the deal, it was considered the second-largest take-over in history.[44] With Disney's purchase of one of the "big three" television networks, they greatly expanded their empire and brought a bit of diversity to their portfolio.

There were numerous advantages to owning ABC. Obviously, it gave Disney ownership across even more entertainment mediums. Disney, already proficient in films, now owned a primary broadcast signal, along with deeper penetration into cable television, as ABC was the owner of several cable networks:

Lifetime, A&E, the History Channel, and others—and, of course, the crown jewel, ESPN.

Disney was already in the sports business before bringing ESPN into their family. Just two months before assuming control of ESPN, Disney bought a 25 percent stake in the California Angels baseball team. This purchase added to the ownership they already had of the NHL's Anaheim Mighty Ducks franchise in 1993.

The acquisition of ABC also afforded Disney the opportunity to get into the radio business. On November 18, 1996, Radio Disney debuted on the ABC Radio Networks. The media onslaught of Disney was ramping up. Disney now had a significant presence in nearly every facet of entertainment—movies, television, radio, news reporting, sports, and, pretty soon, this new thing called the World Wide Web.

February 22, 1996

Disney goes online and launches Disney.com.

OK, let's hop in the Wayback Machine and revisit the days of Netscape Navigator, AOL, Prodigy, AltaVista, Lycos, HotBot, CompuServe, ISPs, and dial-up modems—if you're under twenty-five years old, there's a good chance that none of these words look all that familiar to you!

These are a few of the names associated with the World Wide Web during the mid-1990s. And in early 1996, Disney joined the party and went on the net with Disney.com. By June of 1996, in typical Disney fashion, the website was already garnering 2.5 million hits a day.[45]

Today, Disney.com is still one of the most visited sites in the world, especially by families. From their home page, you can go off to countless other Disney sites and do everything from booking your Disney vacation to receiving parenting advice, from making dining reservations to playing games and watching videos—it's a never-ending labyrinth of Disney promotion.

But what was percolating back in 1996 for Disney Online? In those days, only about ten million folks actively used the Internet, and roughly thirty-five million utilized e-mail.[45]

Well, ever the trendsetter, Disney bucked convention in this new medium and created a website that charged visitors for its content. The site was called

Disney's Daily Blast, and charging for content was a bit taboo back in those days.

In August of 1997, *Computer World* magazine ran a story on the website. Let's see what they had to say about it.

> On its Disney's Daily Blast site, the $18.7 billion giant is breaking a couple of the cardinal rules of consumer-based online commerce: namely that consumers won't pay for online entertainment and that companies should develop a simple site that's accessible to the lowest common denominator of computing hardware and software in order to attract the broadest possible audience.
>
> Disney charges a $4.95 per month subscription fee and requires users to have state-of-the-art technology to access the site. To view the site, consumers need a Pentium-class or higher PC running Windows 95 and a 28.8K-bit/sec modem. An Apple Computer, Macintosh version of the site is due next month, but it will have similar high-end requirements. The site also requires more than 2M bytes of multi-media plug-ins to view.
>
> John Robb, an analyst at Gomez Advisors in Boston, said the strategy is risky. Despite brisk sales in high-end multi-media systems recently, many consumers are still accessing the Internet from 486-based systems and 14.4K bit/sec. modems through online services such as America Online and Compuserve. "Disney's made a choice. The market they're going for is relatively small, but they tend to be leading edge folks—only 3 or 4 million people."
>
> The Daily Blast site is an online service for kids age 12 and under. It offers animated storybooks, downloadable games, educational toys and puzzles, and sports and news written and reported by children.
>
> Disney Online also provides several sites for free, including www.disney.com the company's marketing orientated site, a parenting site, and sites affiliated with the Disney-owned ABC TV network.

The free www.disney.com consistently ranks in the Internet ratings as one of the most popular sites. But it is Daily Blast that is the centerpiece of the Disney Online operation and where Disney is taking the biggest risk—charging a subscription. The overwhelming majority of the sites on the Internet are free, and those that charge subscriptions—such as *The Wall Street Journal*—are seeing uncertain results. Microsoft Corp was in the spotlight when it postponed indefinitely plans to charge online subscriptions for its webzine, *Slate*.

Jake Winebaum, president of Disney Online, said his company is confident that if it builds sufficient, high-quality content into the site, Disney will be able to overcome consumers' resistance to paying for World Wide Web content.[46]

The Disney Blast website was a success for Disney. In June of 1999, Disney merged the Blast site with Disney.com to streamline their web presence. Disney still offered premium content subscriptions but expanded their websites and offerings to all users.

As trends and technology evolve, so does Disney, and with the advent and popularity of apps and less concentration on visiting homepages, Disney segues right into this marketplace without skipping a beat.

Our next story, believe it or not, also has an interesting Internet caveat to it. Get ready for your opportunity to live really close to Mickey Mouse, in your Disney domicile.

June 18, 1996

The first family moves into their new home in Celebration, Florida.

Seriously, who doesn't dream about living at Walt Disney World, or Disneyland, from time to time? Before the mid-1990s, the only person who was able to live this dream was Walt, when he spent time at his apartment above the firehouse on Main Street at Disneyland.

Early into the Decade of Disney, in 1991, Michael Eisner announced plans to do what no previous Disney regime had been able to do: build a residential community on Walt Disney World property.[49]

Disney's plan wasn't just for a few subdivisions and maybe some condos or townhouses. Their project was to build an entire planned community—homes, shops, an office complex, a hospital, and a school system. It would be called Celebration.

Now, this wouldn't be just *any* planned community, of course. We're dealing with Disney, so there was naturally going to be a theme. Since the Walt Disney Company is the world's largest purveyor of nostalgia, the setting for Celebration had to be a community of yesterday.

If a stroll down Main Street, USA, at a Disney park seemed swell, then surely submerging yourself in this setting as a homeowner would be even better.

As Disney had already experimented with in their theme parks, why take a chance trying to create the future when it is so much easier to replicate the past—a place where people can wax nostalgic? To most of us, yesterday always seems so much simpler and less stressful—whether it's accurate or not.

The days of white picket fences, spotless neighborhoods, and friendly neighbors were going to be the standard for Celebration.

Disney's marketing for the community played on the clichés of Norman Rockwell paintings or *The Andy Griffith Show*. As one advertisement stated: "A new American town of Fourth of July parades and school bake sales… spaghetti dinners and fireflies in jars"[50]

As Michael Eisner commented before construction commenced, "We looked at what made communities great in the past, added what we've learned from the best practices today and combined that with a vision and hope for strong communities in the future."[51]

A strong community *in* the future, as Eisner said, not a community *of* the future, as Walt had wanted. However, by bringing this community to fruition, Disney would in many ways finally release themselves from the original EPCOT wishes of Walt, and everyone at the company knew it.

> Today, Disney executives from Michael Eisner, the company's chairman, on down speak of Celebration as the fulfillment of Walt Disney's old dream to build a City on a Hill—a model held up to the world.

"Eisner was very clear from the beginning that he didn't want to do just another residential community," Bob Shinn said over dinner downtown at Max's I. Shinn is senior vice president of Walt Disney Imagineering, giving him responsibility for the company's operations in Florida.

"With Celebration, we're giving something back, trying to blaze a trail to improve American family life, education, and health. This project allows us to fulfill Walt's idea for a town of tomorrow."

Of course, fulfilling the founder's vision was not the only motivation for building Celebration: if it is a City on a Hill, it is at the same time an element in a larger corporate strategy and, very simply, a $2.5 billion real-estate deal, a creative way of packaging and selling Florida swampland. (Disney paid approximately $200 an acre for this land in the 60s; it is selling quarter-acre lots at Celebration for upward of $80,000.)

According to Tom Lewis, perhaps the Disney executive most closely involved with Celebration's early planning, the town had its more earthly origins on Wall Street, in the bloody battle for control of Disney in the early 80s. Part of what made the corporation such an attractive takeover target was the vast acreage of undeveloped real estate it owned in Orlando—the theme parks and hotels occupied only a small fraction of the company's 27,000-acre holdings.

After Michael Eisner took over the company in 1984, he ordered a study of the real estate that determined that some 10,000 acres of it, lying on the south side of Route 192, would never be needed by Walt Disney World. Developing that land in some way would render Disney that much less attractive to a raider.

Another consideration was the fact that Disney's relations with local governments in central Florida had grown somewhat strained. Walt Disney World occupies a state chartered and virtually sovereign municipality called the Reedy Creek Improvement District, which contributes relatively little in the way of taxes to Osceola County, one of the two counties it straddles. By "de-annexing" the 10,000 acres and populating them with taxpayers, Disney could please local governments and smooth the approval process for future theme-park projects, like its new Animal Kingdom. (Had Celebration remained within Reedy Creek, it would also have given Disney's private municipality something it can't afford to have: independent voters.)[52]

Disney built a preview center to provide information about their grand project. Over three months' time, from August to October, over fifteen thousand people visited the center. The public's interest in Celebration was very strong. So strong in fact, that Disney decided to create a lottery system to determine who would have the opportunity to purchase a home site.[53]

On November 18, 1995, roughly five thousand people arrived for the lottery drawing. A $1,000 refundable deposit was needed to enter the lottery and have an opportunity at one of the first 475 homes being built. With the results of the lottery determined, it would only be a matter of months before families began moving into the $2.5 billion project a few miles away from Walt Disney World in the summer of 1996.[53]

When all phases of construction were complete, Disney expected the community would be home to roughly twenty thousand people (as of the 2010 census, the population was around seven thousand). In 1996, house prices ranged from $120,000 to under $1 million. The homes were constructed with touches of modern technology woven into a home that appeared to be from yesterday, and the juxtaposition only gets deeper as you read on.

For decades, the Walt Disney Company used strategic partnerships and sponsorships in their theme parks, and Celebration would be no different. AT&T entered a sponsorship agreement with the community. They would set up a cutting-edge technology infrastructure in the community and donate the equipment to create the Celebration Community Network (CCN). The CCN was a vehicle for the residents to communicate. There was a virtual bulletin board, chat rooms, an e-mail service, and a portal to the Internet. The deal brokered between AT&T and Disney allowed AT&T to utilize the community to test new technology and services. In turn, Disney received the equipment and the creation of the CCN for free.[54]

With the infrastructure in place and residents moving in, it was time to put this technology to use, along with a bit of cyber-snooping 1990s style. For AT&T, the nostalgic community of yesterday was a great façade to collect data on some of its inhabitants.

As mentioned, the Internet wasn't as omnipresent in 1996 as it is today. Long before computer users knew about "cookies," digital footprints, and browser histories, the folks at AT&T were looking to barter with the town's locals. Several families that moved into Celebration became the telecommunication company's guinea pigs.

As AT&T explained, "AT&T wants to understand how people use existing technology, and more important, how you adapt to new and emerging technology, products and services. Our researchers will evaluate and analyze what you use and how you use it over the next year, and your participation will be very valuable in helping us create a model of development for the future."[54]

Translation: Let us bribe you with some free electronics in exchange for monitoring your telecommunication habits. AT&T would enroll the first 350 families to become a part of their study. Participants received a computer (Tandy brand, no less, for all you lovers of electronics produced by that tech giant RadioShack!); a combo printer, copier, and fax machine; a Nokia cellular phone; and landline telephone service. AT&T also covered all fees and bills incurred over a year, something they valued at upward of $3,500.[54]

After a year of using the devices as the primary means to communicate and fully participating in sporadic surveys centered on the technology, the family could keep the equipment. Sounds great—free technology for a few surveys. But in the end, the few surveys weren't that benign.

The devices in the homes were monitored by something called a "Zeus box." The box was placed in the homes to monitor the technology. The box monitored where phone calls went and their duration. On the computer, each website visited and every e-mail sent was logged.

In essence, all the activity on the electronics provided was recorded. The equipment didn't cost the families anything monetarily, as they were paying with their privacy. Zeus wasn't merely tracking what you were doing; there was a bit of information collection with surveys.

Initially, they were mainly about time management via the computer. But as time progressed, they became a bit more interesting. "If given the opportunity would you watch an execution on the Internet? If you could lie or cheat on the Internet without getting caught, would you? Have you ever been embarrassed by anything you've done on the Internet?"[54]

These questions, while still intrusive, seem a bit benign today, as we all know what the Internet evolved into and what sorts of things may be found on it. But for 1996, they seem a bit bizarre coming from a telecommunications company supposedly interested in technology.

So, what did it all mean? Other than the fact that some families are willing to give up their privacy for free technology, no idea. About eight months into the project, it unraveled. The divisions that were going to use the collected data were sold off midway through the program. While AT&T still collected the data, the word is they didn't end up utilizing any of it.

The program was an interesting one. Especially in view of how we now value our online privacy and the pervasiveness of the Internet in all facets of our day-to-day lives.

Well, the Zeus box was obviously short-lived, but the community of Celebration was not. Was it a success? Did it fulfill the original dream of EPCOT? Well, it depends on whom you ask. Just like every other community in the world, there are positives and negatives. In the broad sense, it is a self-contained planned town, which is what EPCOT was going to be in its most general terms.

Today, Celebration is known as the town Disney built. As originally planned, in 2004 Disney divested its stake in the community. They relinquished control over the eighteen acres of land that encompasses shops, restaurants, offices, and homes to Lexin Capital, a private real-estate investment firm.

Next time you're at WDW, it's worth a quick trip over to the community, as it is a cute, quaint little slice of Americana.

April 22, 1998

Disney's Animal Kingdom opens at Walt Disney World.

"Nature is perhaps the greatest storyteller of all. Welcome to the kingdom of animals; real, ancient and imagined. A kingdom ruled by lions, dinosaurs, and dragons; a kingdom of balance, harmony and survival."[55]

These are the words Michael Eisner read during the dedication of Disney's Animal Kingdom when it opened on Earth Day in April of 1998.

The Animal Kingdom isn't just any old Disney park with an animal-centric theme. And as Disney will remind you, it isn't a zoo. The park goes deeper than merely showcasing animals behind bars. The park's theme is a bit more subtle but visible if you look for it: conservation—the respect for diversity of life on mother earth.

The foundation of conservation, education, and environmental awareness seen throughout Disney's Animal Kingdom works in tandem with the Disney Conservation Fund. The fund was established on Earth Day in 1995, and over the past twenty-plus years has contributed $40 million in the form of grants to support 330 nonprofit organizations. Also, the fund has helped to protect more than four hundred different species of animals and inspired millions of kids and families to explore the great outdoors.[56]

Animal altruism aside, this wasn't the first time Walt Disney World was home to more than a mouse. In April of 1974, Disney opened their second attraction separate from the Magic Kingdom. It was originally called Treasure Island and later renamed Discovery Island.[63]

The island was an eleven-acre aviary / bird sanctuary / small zoo, smack dab in the middle of Bay Lake near the Magic Kingdom. During the late 1970s, the island was home to over three hundred different species of birds—admission in 1979 was $1.50 for an adult and $0.75 for children.[64]

In addition to birds, there were several exhibits on plants, animals, gators, and Galapagos turtles. Discovery Island educated visitors on conservation efforts, breeding, and research. During the early 1980s, the island attempted to save the endangered dusky seaside sparrow, to no avail.[63]

In 1987, Disney had a new project for Discovery Island. The island collaborated with the nonprofit organization Helping Hands: Simian Aides for the Disabled. The group placed trained monkeys in homes with disabled people.

Helping Hands: Simian Aides for the Disabled put their colony of fifty-three capuchin monkeys (often called organ-grinder monkeys) in a specially created breeding colony on Discovery Island. Disney provided the organization with a training and breeding facility for the animals before they went into homes to help those in need.[62]

By 1998, when the nearly $800 million, five-hundred-acre Animal Kingdom park debuted, it was difficult for Discovery Island to compete against this behemoth. In 1999, twenty-five years after the park opened, it closed its doors.

Gone but not forgotten. Today, Disney's Animal Kingdom gives a nod to the animal park of yesterday with a region of the park aptly named Discovery Island.

This part of the park is just one of the many exciting areas of the Animal Kingdom. To the left of Discovery Island is the African region of the park, and to the right is the Asian area. Both parts of the park feature a portion of nearly two thousand different animals across three hundred species.

Disney went to great lengths to ensure a safe, pleasant environment and habitat for the animals. Disney assembled an excellent advisory board, who were cognizant of the limitations and delicate nature of creating an "animal kingdom." The last thing Disney wanted was to have a situation similar to Sea World's, where animal or trainer deaths would provide fuel for animal-rights activists to create negative publicity for the park.

Disney's board consists of consultants and members of animal and wildlife protection groups, zoologists, curators from the world's top zoo's, and, most notably, legendary primatologist Jane Goodall.

Disney's Animal Kingdom opened to the usual fanfare and media attention that we know is the standard practice for a Disney park opening. And with what has become somewhat of a standard of this book's coverage of a Disney park opening, we will check out a member of the media's perspective of the opening festivities.

This article focuses more on Disney's "marketing machine" during the inauguration of a new park, the lengths the company goes to, and the millions spent on promoting their new investment.

> When Walt Disney World opens Animal Kingdom, its fourth theme park, it will feed, house and entertain a herd of thousands. But they won't be the exotic animals that will roam over the re-creation of an African savannah.
>
> Disney will play host to about 5,000 media, industry analysts, travel planners and corporate partners at the April 22 opening

of the $800 million attraction. In return, the company will get wide coverage in newspapers and on television, feedback to investors and first-person testimonials by travel experts.

Disney will pay the tab for airfare, hotel rooms and meals of many of the invited guests—about half of whom are expected to be journalists.

"They do it a lot, and they do get a lot of bang for their buck," said Tim O'Brien, an editor at Amusement Business, a theme park trade magazine.

Although Disney won't say how much it is spending on the public relations affair, it's expected to be well into the millions.

Although it's expensive, it helps that many of the costs for the celebration are in-house. Disney has a partnership with Delta Airlines, which will fly in guests from around the world at discounted prices. The guests say at one of Disney's 17 resort hotels and eat at Disney restaurants.

Because many media organizations forbid their workers from accepting freebies, Disney is offering discounted packages for some reporters. For $550, a reporter gets three nights in a Disney hotel, three meals a day and three days' worth of passes to Disney theme parks. For an extra $200, they get flown in from anywhere in the United States.

Ordinarily, such a package without airfare would cost at least $835 for one person, according to Disney's central reservation office. Disney is raising individual ticket prices to theme parks for ordinary people by $2 to $44.52 after Animal Kingdom opens.[57]

My, how the world of promotion has grown over the decades for Disney. Remember, this was still long before everyone had an Internet-equipped device attached to his or her hip, where virtually anyone could be a member of the press via a blog or website.

Disney's Animal Kingdom opened to positive reviews and long lines in 1998, but for many keen observers of Disney, the park opened without one thing: the Beastly Kingdom.

When Michael Eisner announced the creation of the park in June of 1995, he painted a slightly different picture of the park.

> "A celebration of animals that ever or never existed. Disney's Wild Animal Kingdom will be magical, fanciful and fun in the tradition of all of our theme parks, yet it will incorporate a new dimension of reality with live animals in their natural habitats."

> The park would ultimately include themed "lands" connected by a central hub: Africa, which takes visitors on a safari with live, wild animals; the Beastly Kingdom focusing on mythological creatures, like unicorns and dragons; and Dinoland, with dinosaurs and extinct species brought to life through robotics.[58]

> The proposed Beastly Kingdom was to be filled with storybook animals. Top draw is Dragon's Tower, a suspended roller coaster ride through a wrecked castle inhabited by a fire breathing dragon. Quest of the Unicorn Maze. Musical boat rides past the dancing hippos from Disney's *Fantasia*.[59]

It appears as though the Beastly Kingdom made its way into the discarded Disney file, as this region of the park never came to be. However, in 2011, Disney put a plan in motion to bring another fantastic fantasy world to the Animal Kingdom.[60]

Disney signed a licensing agreement with James Cameron to bring Pandora to life from Cameron's blockbuster movie *Avatar*. Disney broke ground in this region of the Animal Kingdom in 2014. It will certainly bring a new level of fantasy to the park.[61]

The 1990s were a busy decade for Disney. While the company didn't conquer all of their plans outlined in Eisner's Decade of Disney project, the company did see near-unprecedented growth not seen since the days of Walt Disney himself. Disney not only solidified their status again as a major player and trendsetter in the film industry, but they ventured into some new arenas with a planned community, network television ownership, a cruise line, and runaway expansion at Walt Disney World.

Here are a few more highlights from the 1990s.

April 1, 1995: Blizzard Beach water park debuts at WDW.

October 1, 1995: The Disney Channel debuts in the United Kingdom.

March 28, 1997: Disney's Wide World of Sports complex debuts at WDW.

September 15, 1997: Downtown Disney West Side opens at WDW.

March 23, 1998: *ESPN the Magazine* is published.

June 19, 1998: The feature film *Mulan* is released.

July 30, 1998: The Disney Magic cruise ship departs on its inaugural voyage.

January 15, 1999: The All-Star Movies Resort opens at WDW.

CHAPTER EIGHT

2000S

The last chapter of *The Disney Story* is upon us, as is the new millennium. While some in the world may have been preoccupied with the "end of days," as Y2K offered good fodder for the media, Disney worked to extend their entertainment domination into a new Disney decade.

Many of the projects Disney started in the late nineties were coming to an end early in the new millennium—as was the tenure of the project's chief architect. The savior of the mouse was beginning to outstay his welcome.

History often repeats itself, and in this situation, the parallels were uncanny. It was starting to look like 1984 all over again for Disney, as another corporate giant was becoming very fond of Mickey.

Change was on the horizon in the kingdom of Disney, but before a new king could be coronated, the original kingdom was finally receiving a new addition.

February 8, 2001

Disney's California Adventure opens adjacent to Disneyland.

Where: Adjacent to Disneyland. Size: Fifty-five acres. Construction costs: $1.4 billion. Price of admission opening year: $43 for adults, $30 for children ages three to nine. Park capacity: thirty-three thousand people. Parking capacity: ten thousand vehicles. Workers needed to staff to park: 7,500. Theme: The state of California's history and natural wonders. Major attractions: Some new experiences and old favorites found at other Disney parks—Soarin' over California, California Screamin', Grizzly River Run, It's Tough to Be a Bug!, Muppet Vision 3D, and Downtown Disney, among other attractions.[1]

After nearly fifty years of solitude, Disneyland finally had a sibling next door, and, on paper, it sounded great. Perhaps not as great as what Disney had proposed in 1991 and won Anaheim's approval for in 1993, but it would suffice.[2]

The original plan for Disneyland's second attraction was Westcot, the West Coast's version of Epcot. The proposed project would run Disney about $2.75 billion and would contain 4,600 hotel rooms, a five-thousand-seat amphitheater, a shopping area, and, of course, a version of the Epcot theme park.[3]

Ultimately, rather than create competition next door to Disneyland, the company took a different approach: complement the legendary park rather than dwarf it. Also, the financial struggles of Disneyland Paris helped to dismantle the Westcot plan.[2]

In turn, Disney built a park with more modest expectations. Barry Braverman, Imagineering executive producer for the park, commented, "It was planned to enhance, not compete with the Disneyland experience. Disneyland is a classic; it's the original, and it's had over 45 years to evolve. We wanted the sister park to be a different kind of place, telling a different story"[4]

Disneyland spokeswoman Michele Nachum took it even further when she commented about having two parks at Disneyland, offering an experience similar to that of Walt Disney World. "We think Disneyland is now a three-to-four day experience."[4]

The yearly attendance projections weren't grand for Disney's California Adventure. The target number for annual attendance hovered around the seven million mark, which is roughly half what Disneyland would draw annually, give or take a million or two.[5]

But when the park debuted and was consistently drawing in the neighborhood of nine thousand to twelve thousand guests a day, Disney was less than thrilled with this performance.[6]

Critics and visitors panned the park. Many complained the park lacked imagination and that there wasn't enough to do, especially for kids. Overall, many folks didn't think it was worth the price of admission.

The summer after the park opened, Disney dropped the price of admission by ten dollars and offered free admission to one child accompanied by an adult.[6]

Before the end of the first year, Disney heard the complaints and worked to reshape the park. They brought in the characters from the hit movie *Monsters,*

Inc. to mingle with the crowd; replaced a vegetable garden with A Bug's Land, based on the hit movie *A Bug's Life*; and started to recreate the hugely popular Twilight Zone Tower of Terror that thrilled guests at WDW's Hollywood Studios. The park even saw a change in menu, with more kid-friendly options for dining.

At the park's one-year anniversary, five million people visited. It didn't reach the targeted seven million, but it wasn't the attendance bomb the park started out to be.[7] Not to mention that the tragedies of September 11, 2001 affected all domestic travel and vacations, and each of Disney's parks saw a drop in attendance in the months after the attacks.

As time progressed, Disney's California Adventure still lagged, and Disney reworked the park again. In 2007, Disney announced an expansion on the horizon. Coming soon, Buena Vista Street and Cars Land, among other new attractions. As the new regions of the park debuted, attendance began to increase steadily.

In 2014, the park's attendance surpassed the 7 million mark with 8.7 million visitors, and in 2015, attendance rose to 9.3 million visitors.[8] It is not easy being second fiddle.

September 4, 2001

Tokyo's DisneySea theme park opens.

In the summer of 1990, Disney submitted a master plan to the city of Long Beach in California for the company's proposed $1 billion waterfront resort and theme park, Port Disney.[9]

The project would be adjacent to the port of Long Beach and would feature hotels, shopping, restaurants, and the world's largest aquarium. Not to mention the Disney-owned ship, the Queen Mary, and the Spruce Goose, built by Howard Hughes—and, of course, you can't forget the all-important theme park, DisneySea.[9]

By 1992, Port Disney was scrapped when the government of California didn't seem too interested in contributing to the project. Also, the mess Disney was dealing with over in France with Euro Disney didn't help things.[10]

So instead of Disney in Long Beach, the company repurposed the project and announced, in November of 1992, that components of Port Disney would be featured as the second attraction alongside Tokyo Disneyland.[10]

It took a few years for Disney and their Japanese partner, Oriental Land Company, to work out the logistics and details of the park, and in November of 1997, the particulars of the park were announced.

Disney entered into a licensing agreement with Oriental Land Company similar to when Tokyo Disneyland was built. Oriental Land would own and operate the park, with Disney collecting royalties and fees for their intellectual property and consulting services.[11]

DisneySea, as the park's name alludes to, is a nautical-themed park. On opening day, the park featured twenty-three attractions over 176 acres, and, much like Tokyo Disneyland, it is a highly successful park today.

In 2015, the park's attendance topped 13.6 million people, just 3 million shy of its neighbor, Tokyo Disneyland, and roughly 2 million more than WDW's Epcot.[11]

The Disney theme parks are a major success in Japan. The folks in the country fully embrace not only Disney but also American culture. Before Disney parks set up shop in Japan, the country never celebrated Halloween; this is according to a press release Disney put out in September of 2004.[12]

> "Ask any native, and they will tell you that less than 10 years ago, Halloween was non-existent. But that did not stop the Imagineers and entertainment specialists from producing elaborate Halloween events that today are one of the biggest drivers of visitation to the Disney resort.
>
> In Tokyo, where Disneyland is perceived of as a Western park and Americana is celebrated, we introduced elements of a traditional US Halloween with "trick-or-treating" and guests dressed up in costumes.
>
> So why create a holiday where it didn't exist before? In Japan, the only time Halloween was celebrated was reportedly on the American bases in the 1970s, and although retailers tried to sell spooky merchandise and candy in the 1980s and 1990s,

Halloween did not take off in Japan until the Tokyo Disney Resort started to make waves with their celebration.[12]

Halloween at Tokyo Disneyland was originally a one-day event when it was rolled out in 1998. Today, the celebration spans two months at the park, and it has even permeated Japanese culture beyond the parks, with the holiday quickly becoming a cultural phenomenon across the nation.[13]

Perhaps this is a bit of cultural redemption for Disney. They contributed something positive culturally toward Japan, and the residents embraced it rather than feel as though they were being assaulted by it, something the French often complained about.

November 2, 2001

Monsters Inc. is released.

> I'm the dope who turned down *Toy Story*. Jeffrey Katzenberg brought me over to his house when they were making *Aladdin* and said, "You have to meet this young man." It turned out to be John Lasseter…I thought John was a genius, but I got bad advice from agents and managers, then didn't follow my own instincts. It turned out not happening [for me], and now it's one of the great movies of all time. The next time John called, I picked up the phone and went, "Whatever it is, John, yes!" It turned out to be *Monsters, Inc.*[14]

This is the engaging story of how Billy Crystal became the voice of Mike Wazowski in Pixar's smash hit *Monsters, Inc.* However, there is a more intriguing story about the movie—how it was created one afternoon.

In the summer of 1994, John Lasseter, Andrew Stanton, Joe Ranft, and Pete Docter were having a lunch meeting at the Hidden City Café in Point Richmond, California. The guys from Pixar were discussing what they were going to do next, as *Toy Story* was just about complete. The crew needed to get started on another film, and a brainstorming session commenced during what came to be a pretty legendary lunch—oh, to be a fly on the wall that day!

The creative juices flowed freely that day, as the outlines and characters for four of the studio's greatest movies came together on their lunch napkins: 1998's *A Bug's Life*, 2001's *Monsters Inc.*, 2003's *Finding Nemo*, and 2008's *Wall-E*.[15]

Now there's an excellent example of a power lunch. These four movies have brought in billions of dollars in revenue between the films and merchandise; spawned two sequels, *Monsters University* and *Finding Dory*; and were nominated for fifteen Academy Awards, winning three.[15]

Next time you're watching *Monsters, Inc.*, a sharp eye can catch a scene where Pixar paid tribute to the restaurant, memorializing it forever in Pixar history, as the restaurant closed its doors in 2012.

December 5, 2001

Happy one hundredth birthday, Walt Disney!

March 16, 2002

Walt Disney Studios Park in Paris opens.

The Walt Disney Company loves to merchandise and market their quotes, sayings, and idioms. We've all seen them: "If you can dream it, you can do it." "It's kind of fun to do the impossible." "All our dreams can come true if we have the courage to pursue them." The list goes on and on.

Well, apparently there is one phrase that Disney never heard of: "Don't throw good money after bad," because here we are, in early 2002, with the opening of another park in France.

The opening of Walt Disney Studios Paris coincided with the ten-year anniversary of Disneyland Paris's grand opening. The park's theme is centered on movies and television; as the park's website touts,

> Discover the secrets behind the most magical scenes of Disney film and television at Walt Disney Studios Park. From legendary moments in motion at Toon Studio to the mind-boggling effects of the Backlot, 5 production zones bursting with thrills drop you and your little stars smack bang in the limelight.

The park sounds a bit like the original Disney's MGM Studios at WDW. In fact, much like the early ambitions for that park, Walt Disney Studios in Paris was to have a similar vibe and atmosphere to the park in Florida. Here's a bit of the preview from when Disney announced the park in September of 1999.

> Disney chief Gilles Pelisson said visitors to the park will watch cartoonists at work, attend special effects shows, and watch shoots of TV programs. "The goal is that visitors pass through the movie screen and see what's behind it," Pelisson said. "It's about interaction."
>
> Euro Disney officials also intend for the park to be home to movie shoots and other artistic endeavors. Walt Disney Co. has said it will put up 39 percent of the capital, in keeping with its current commitment to Euro Disney. Once the park is fully operational, the company expects an estimated 4.2 million visitors annually.[16]

Hmm, now it really sounds like the park in Florida. If you recall, back in 1989 Eisner commented that building Disney's MGM Studios would help foster a longer stay at WDW. While the park was successful in tacking on days to a vacation at WDW, the whole working studio concept didn't pan out.

It is interesting to see that Disney would actually give this format a try again, especially knowing the backstory on Disneyland Paris, a park that consistently had trouble paying its bills.

As you can imagine, the park opened, and the attendance numbers were less than stellar, often drawing around two million visitors a year.

Roughly two years after Walt Disney Studios Park opened, the group that operated Disneyland Paris and Walt Disney Studios Park was facing financial ruin again. In June 2004, Euro Disney SCA said it could default on debt payments to the Walt Disney Company and other lenders unless creditors approved a restructuring. The outstanding debt was roughly $2.8 billion.[17]

In September of 2004, Mickey came to the rescue and bailed the park out, restructuring and deferring debt and royalty repayments. Additionally, Disney infused the parks with another $328 million for additions and improvements.[18]

Today, attendance wise, Walt Disney Studios Park settles in at the original projections. In 2015, the park's attendance was 4.4 million people, but financial turmoil still plagues both parks despite being one of the most-visited tourist attractions in all of Europe.[19]

July 9, 2003

Pirates of the Caribbean: Curse of the Black Pearl is released.

In the early 2000s, Disney announced that they were flipping the script on a few of their upcoming movies. Traditionally, Disney released a movie, and, if it was successful, it could eventually end up with a presence in their theme parks, usually in the way of an immersive ride experience.

Well, in 2003, moviegoers got to experience three Disney feature films where the catalyst for the story was rooted in a theme park attraction.

The Country Bears was based on the Country Bear Jamboree, and *The Haunted Mansion* and *Pirates of the Caribbean: Curse of the Black Pearl* were based on the legendary theme park attractions.[20]

Of the three movies, *Pirates of the Caribbean* is by far the most successful. When the film was released in the summer of 2003, it had a $46.4 million opening weekend and took in nearly $71 million during its first week.[21]

These figures made the summer box office quite lucrative for Disney, as *Finding Nemo* was released on May 30, 2003 and was an enormous success in its own right—at the time, *Nemo* became Disney's highest-grossing animated film.

By the end of the summer, *Nemo* had grossed over $330 million, and Captain Jack Sparrow came in with $261 million in domestic box office sales. *Pirates* cost the studio $135 million to produce, so obviously, the film was profitable after just the first summer.[22]

The success of *Pirates* extended much further than the box office of 2003, as this film sparked an entire franchise of *Pirates of the Caribbean* movies. Jerry Bruckheimer and Johnny Depp turned one of the last rides Walt Disney had worked on before he passed away into a five-film, multibillion-dollar series. Not too bad, considering Bruckheimer, the producer, had his reservations about doing the movie.

"Initially, Mr. Bruckheimer said, he did not want to make *Pirates* because it is based on the Disneyland ride of the same name, and 'rides aren't my thing.' But he was persuaded to proceed after he found that he could hire Ted Elliott and Terry Rossio, two of the writers of *Shrek*, to revise the script."[23]

Good move, Jerry!

December 14, 2003

The Pop Century Resort opens at Walt Disney World.

No American company is more fluent in pop culture than the Walt Disney Company. Heck, they helped define the subject decades ago and refine it each and every year.

After working in the medium for many decades, it is no surprise that Disney chose to theme a resort at WDW on pop culture.

To be honest, Disney didn't need to create and model a hotel after twentieth-century pop culture, as two of their hotels were the settings for monumental events during the 1970s that contributed immensely to the subject.

Our first Disney hotel pop-culture event is with President Richard Nixon, at Walt Disney World's Contemporary Resort on November 19, 1973.

President Nixon was no stranger to the world of Disney. Over his career in politics as president and vice president of the United States, Nixon and Walt Disney became quite familiar with each other.

Not long after Disneyland opened in 1955, then vice president Nixon visited the park with his family and was presented with a ceremonial key to Disneyland. In 1959, he returned to help inaugurate the Disneyland Monorail. In 1969, after Walt's death, Nixon awarded Walt's widow and family the Walt Disney Commemorative Medal—Walt received the Presidential Medal of Freedom in 1964, but President Johnson bestowed that honor upon him.[24]

President Nixon is, of course, also present at Walt Disney World's Hall of Presidents. But perhaps his most memorable Disney performance took place at a Disney hotel when he addressed hundreds of members of the Associated Press Managing Editors Association.

During this meeting, Nixon was embroiled in the Watergate scandal, and he "wanted the facts out, because the facts will prove that the president is telling the truth."[25]

As the president tried to clear his name during a heated question-and-answer situation with the press, he gave this legendary quote: "In all of my years in public life I have never obstructed justice...People have got to know whether or not their president is a crook. Well, I'm not a crook."[25]

On August 9, 1974, Richard Nixon resigned as president of the United States.

Now, let us take a quick trip on the WDW monorail and head over to Disney's Polynesian Village during Christmastime of 1974.

Just before the new year of 1975, one of the members of the Fab Four broke hearts everywhere when he crushed any hope of the Beatles getting back together.

May Pang, who at the time was dating John Lennon, chronicled the moment in her book *Instamatic Karma*. John was originally supposed to sign the legal documents dismantling the legendary band in New York City.

After commenting that the "stars weren't right," John skipped the meeting in New York and headed to Florida. On December 29, 1974, the band's lawyers traveled to WDW and met John at WDW's Polynesian Village. Lennon signed his name to the documents ending the band's reign.[26]

And there you have it: two actual pop-culture moments from a WDW hotel, not dreamed up by Imagineers and featured at Disney's Pop Century Resort!

September 12, 2005

Hong Kong Disneyland debuts.

OK, so we established a few pages back that perhaps Disney wasn't too fond of the phrase "throw good money after bad" when it came to their experience in France. However, they did learn from some of their mistakes at Disneyland Paris, most notably how to tactfully meld the magic and Americana of Disney into local cultures.

So how does Disney spell redemption for their gaffes in France? H-O-N-G K-O-N-G. This time, Disney did their homework and executed a perfect assimilation of their world into an ancient and complex world.

> "Paris taught us that we always have to listen to our consumers to be sure the park fits within their cultures and desires," said Jay Rasulo, president of Walt Disney Parks & Resorts. Thus, Mickey, Donald, and Goofy will need to learn two Chinese dialects. "We do find that children like to be greeted in their own language," Rasulo said. "Our park will be trilingual with English, Cantonese and Mandarin."[27]

Jay Rasulo gave the above quote to the *New York Times* in 2003, when Disney broke ground on Hong Kong Disneyland. A trilingual park was a drop in the cultural bucket for Disney. The park is one of the smaller Disney theme parks, but the attention to detail and sensitivity to Chinese culture, particularly feng shui, make this park truly unique.

Chinese culture is steeped in tradition, symbolism, superstition, and nature. One practice that dates back more than three thousand years is feng shui ("feng" means "wind," and "shui" means "water"). This tradition is the art of placing objects in harmony with one another to improve health, prosperity, and luck.

According to an article from the *New York Times* titled "The Feng Shui Kingdom," Disney was mindful of the intricate details of feng shui and numerology when creating Hong Kong Disneyland.

> When building the new entrance to Hong Kong Disneyland, Walt Disney executives decided to shift the angle of the front gate by 12 degrees. They did so after consulting a feng shui specialist, who said the change would ensure prosperity for the park. Disney also put a bend in the walkway from the train station to the gate, to make sure the flow of positive energy, or chi, did not slip past the entrance and out to the China Sea.

> Heeding the advice of a feng shui consultant is one of many steps Disney executives have taken at the park to reflect the local culture—and to make sure they do not repeat some mistakes of the past.

> Some of the dazzling visual effects and nods to cultural differences at Hong Kong Disneyland may seem like so much marketing. One of the park's main ballrooms, which will surely be used for Disney's popular wedding services, measures 888 square meters, because 8 is thought to be a number of fortune, said Wing Chao, who is the master planner of architecture and design at Walt Disney Imagineering. In Chinese, the number four is considered bad luck so there are no fourth-floor buttons in the elevators at the Hollywood Hotel or other hotels in the park.

Cash registers are close to corners or along walls, where such placement is believed to increase prosperity. And in the park's upscale restaurant, Crystal Lotus, Disney installed a virtual koi pond where computer-animated fish dart away from guests who walk on a glass screen. The pond is one of five feng shui elements in the restaurant; the others are wood, earth, metal, and fire, which glows on a screen behind bottles in the bar. "We could not have real fire because of the fire code," said Mr. Chao.[28]

Creating a culturally sensitive Hong Kong Disneyland goes deeper than numerology and feng shui. Disney was even cognizant of colors, merchandise, and queues.

The color red in Chinese culture is symbolic of prosperity, so Disney was sure to include this color where appropriate.

On the other end of the spectrum is green, most notably a green hat. In Chinese lore, a man wearing a green hat symbolizes that his spouse has committed adultery—we're looking at you, Peter Pan. A quick survey of the attractions at Hong Kong Disneyland reveals Peter Pan's flight and his green cap are absent from the Fantasyland area of the park.[29]

So you won't be shopping for a Peter Pan hat at the park, and you also won't be able to purchase a Mickey Mouse clock either—or any clock, for that matter. A Chinese superstition says giving a clock as a gift is a bad omen and insinuates that one will go to a funeral.[29]

OK, no green hats, lots of red, sensitivity to numbers and feng shui. Are we missing anything? Yes, one more thing: how to wait in line, or lack thereof.

When Hong Kong Disneyland opened its doors in 2005, many visitors complained of two-hour waits for an attraction. One guest said he was in the park for twelve hours and only managed to experience four rides. Some of the wait times were due to the newness of the park, but most felt the issues had more to do with visitors from mainland China who were unaccustomed to waiting in line.

Apparently, there are even cultural differences when it comes to waiting in line or queuing, and, of course, there is someone out there who studies it. Let's read about what plagued Hong Kong Disneyland in the early months of the park.

Some Hong Kong residents say the problems were made worse by pushing and shoving by mainland Chinese visitors unaccustomed to orderly waiting.

There are, in fact, cultural differences in how people behave while in line, according to social scientists and park designers. Those differences have even led to physical changes in so-called queuing areas at some parks.

Rongrong Zhou, an assistant professor of marketing at Hong Kong University of Science and Technology, said the differences went beyond a Hong Kong–mainland split. Ms. Zhou, who has studied the psychology of queuing in Hong Kong, said there was a tendency among Asians and others in more collective cultures to compare their situation with those around them. This may make it more likely that they will remain in a line even if it is excessively long.

Ms. Zhou said this finding was rooted in a somewhat paradoxical observation: that it is the people behind a person in line, rather than in front, that determines the person's behavior.

"The likelihood of people giving up and leaving the queue is lower when they see more people behind them," Ms. Zhou said. "You feel like you are in a better position than the others behind you."

By contrast, she said, Americans and others in more individualistic societies make fewer "social comparisons" of this sort. They don't necessarily feel better that more people are behind them but feel bad if too many people are in front of them. Lines in these cultures tend to be more self-limiting.

In a place like Hong Kong, however, the lines may just grow and grow. "The longer the line, people think the service is more worthwhile to get," Ms. Zhou said.

Jay Rasulo, chairman of Walt Disney Parks and Resorts, said that in the first few weeks of the Hong Kong park's operation, officials have noticed more specific differences between Hong Kong visitors and those from the mainland. About 25 percent of Hong Kong residents, Mr. Rasulo said, had already visited a Disney theme park. As a result, he said, they "seem a little more respectful."

Visitors from mainland China, where only 1 percent have visited a Disney park, are still trying to figure out how lines work. "They are not as impulsive" as some of their peers in Europe, he said, but they also are not as patient as the Japanese.

Europeans, Mr. Rasulo, added, "have very different attitudes about how they wait for things." At the Disneyland Resort Paris, while British visitors are orderly, French and Italians "never saw a line they couldn't be in front of."

After the French park opened, Mr. Rasulo said, the company made the lines narrower by moving handrails closer together to try to prevent people from pushing ahead of others.[30]

Lines or no lines, Hong Kong Disney was a culturally correct theme park for Disney. That doesn't mean it made the park a huge financial success overnight, or, for that matter, after a year or two. Attendance has surged and waned over the years. In 2015, the park saw 6.8 million guests, down a million from 2014.[31]

In 2013, Hong Kong Disney finally posted a profit. Disney initially invested $316 million for a 43 percent equity stake in the park; the remaining percentage is owned by the Hong Kong government, which spent over $400 million. With nearly a half a billion invested in their park, surely the government wasn't thrilled when word got out in 2009 that another Disney park was in the works for Mainland China.[32]

October 1, 2005

Robert Iger becomes CEO of the Walt Disney Company.

The timeline above may read 2005, but it's starting to look a bit like 1984 again. In the two years before Robert Iger took over at Disney, the company was rife with infighting, the possibility of another corporate take-over, a shareholder revolt, and a disgruntled Roy E. Disney leading the charge again to oust the very man he had coveted and helped anoint as CEO. Here's how it all went down.

On November 30, 2003, Roy E. Disney abruptly resigned from the company's board of directors and called for Michael Eisner to resign as CEO. Roy's resignation was abrupt but not entirely unfounded, as he had urged Eisner to step down several times but the Disney board didn't back it. Roy was unsatisfied with the direction the company was heading and wanted a change at the top.

His complaints were varied. Roy outlined that Eisner allowed senior executives to leave the company, and more troubling was that the studio's positive relationship with the very profitable Pixar had become strained, primarily due to Eisner.

Roy complained about Eisner's micromanagement style, along with the lack of success by a few of his more recent acquisitions, especially ABC and go.com—not to mention the company's profits were down.

To make matters worse, Roy was unhappy with corporate governance guidelines that called for all directors to retire at age seventy-two—he was seventy-three at the time. Many suggested Roy's resignation was a preemptive move, as the nominating committee failed to recommend him for another term and there was speculation that he would be forced from the board.[33]

With that, Roy drafted a letter and sent it to Eisner, imploring him to leave the company. "It is my sincere belief that it is you who should be leaving and not me. Accordingly, I once again call for your resignation or retirement. The Walt Disney Company deserves fresh, energetic leadership at this challenging time in its history."[33]

Roy took his position and letter public. He created a website, SaveDisney.com, to outline his stance and garner public support for the ouster of the head mouse.[34]

Disney—or shall I say Eisner—fired back when they took out full-page ads touting the Disney brand and Eisner's accomplishments. They implored shareholders and the public not to be misled by others' claims and to stand by their president.[35]

The situation sounds pretty reminiscent of 1984, when Roy stepped down from the board and sought to have Walt's son-in-law Ron Miller removed from his role as president of the company, only a bit nastier and sans the website. Now the only thing missing from this Disney war to complete the comparison with 1984 is a corporate take-over. Cue the Comcast Corporation.

In February of 2004, Comcast Corporation, the nation's largest cable operator, made an unsolicited offer of $54 billion to buy the Walt Disney Company.[36]

Comcast had worked for some time to acquire Disney. They tried working directly with Eisner on a merger, but when little progress was made, they went public with their offer. Comcast sent a letter to the Disney board and the general public outlining the benefits of the merger, stating the collaboration of the two behemoths would restore the Disney brand.[37]

The deal would have created the world's largest entertainment conglomerate— if you think there is already an enormous amount of Disney programming and commercials now, can you imagine what it would have been like if this deal had gone through?

A week later, Disney's board rejected the offer; they felt it was too low. By the end of April 2004, Comcast relented and rescinded their offer.[38]

Eisner may have staved off a corporate take-over, but the pressure of Roy Disney still loomed large, and he wouldn't relent. In March of 2004, at Disney's annual shareholder's meeting, 43 percent of the voting shareholders gave Eisner a "lack of confidence" and stripped him of his chairman title. Eisner would remain CEO, but the title of chairman went to former United States senator and Disney board member George Mitchell.[39, 40]

In the end, Roy prevailed. Eisner announced that he was going to step down on September 30, 2005, a year before his contract expired.[40] Eisner's longtime confidant and second-in-command, Robert Iger, took control of Disney on October 1, 2005, and wasted no time getting down to business. Iger worked to repair the Disney-Disney relationship by reaching out to Roy. He extended an olive branch by offering Roy an office at the Burbank studio, a consultancy position, and the title of director emeritus.[41]

Next, he reached out to Pixar and Steve Jobs. Iger went back to the negotiating table, as the agreement between the two studios was set to expire.

Then, in a move that would make Walt Disney himself jump for joy, Iger brought home a long-lost family member. In February of 2006, Disney announced the return of Oswald the Lucky Rabbit to the Walt Disney Company. Here's what the press release said at the time:

> Disney President and Chief Executive Officer Robert A. Iger announced today the return of Oswald the Lucky Rabbit to The Walt Disney Company by agreement with NBC/Universal, the company that had previously owned the rights to Oswald since his theatrical debut in 1927.

> "As the forerunner to Mickey Mouse and an important part of Walt Disney's creative legacy, the fun and mischievous Oswald is back where he belongs, at the home of his creator and among the stable of beloved characters created by Walt himself," said Iger.

> "When Bob was named CEO, he told me he wanted to bring Oswald back to Disney, and I appreciate that he is a man of his word," said Walt Disney's daughter, Diane Disney Miller. "Having Oswald around again is going to be a lot of fun."

> When Walt Disney opened his animation studio in 1923, he spent four years producing The Alice Comedies, a popular series of shorts featuring a live girl in a cartoon world. After four years, Walt created a new character—Oswald the Lucky Rabbit. Walt produced 26 Oswald cartoons, which were distributed by Universal and well-received by audiences. However, on a trip to New York to renew his contract for Oswald, Walt discovered a clause in his contract that gave Universal ownership of his popular new character. On the train ride back to Hollywood, Walt was devastated but realized he needed to create a new character— one that he would entirely own—and during that long trip across country, Mickey Mouse was born.

> The transfer of ownership is part of an agreement permitting sportscaster Al Michaels to contract with NBC. In the transaction ESPN also acquired significant programming and promotional rights, including telecast rights to the live Friday coverage of four Ryder Cup golf championships through 2014, expanded video highlights for the Olympics through 2012, video promotion for ESPN's Monday Night Football

during NBC's Sunday night football through 2011, and expanded highlight rights for other NBC Sports properties through 2011.[42]

Iger was off and running as king of the Disney kingdom. Regardless of how embattled Eisner's last few years had been at the helm of the company, he left enormous shoes to fill. He had added sports teams, a cruise line, several theme parks, a network television channel, ten cable channels, retail stores, Broadway shows, thousands of hotels at Walt Disney World, renewed domination and stability on the studio front, and, what usually matters most, he padded the bottom line. Under Eisner, Disney saw annual profits rise from $291 million to $1.85 billion, and the stock soared 3,598 percent. And in the process, he made himself a billionaire. Not too shabby for two decades' work.[43]

January 20, 2006

High School Musical airs on the Disney Channel.

When the romantic teen comedy/musical debuted on the Disney Channel in early 2006, it broke all Disney channel records for viewers. The night of the premiere, eight million people tuned in. The next evening, it grabbed another six million viewers. Disney even aired a karaoke version, allowing those at home to sing along. With overnight success like that, a franchise was born.[44]

The movie soundtrack went multiplatinum and eventually landed at the top of the *Billboard* charts. *High School Musical* was even the first full-length film to be sold via digital download, on Apple's iTunes Music Store—how's that for a trivia question![45]

High School Musical was to the mid-2000s what Davy Crockett was to the mid-50s—a pop-culture phenomenon that provided Disney with a cottage industry unto itself.

The movie was seen by over a hundred million people worldwide, and it eventually launched a concert tour, several sequels, countless types of merchandise, and a few careers—most notably Zac Efron, Vanessa Hudgins, and Ashley Tisdale.

March 24, 2006

Hannah Montana made her debut on the Disney Channel.

Still riding the success of *High School Musical*, Disney unleashed onto the world Miley Cyrus, a.k.a. Hannah Montana, on the Disney Channel. The show, geared toward the tween set, went down the same road as *High School Musical*, with incredible ratings and a loyal fan base that pined for anything from the show. The Disney marketing machine pumped out multiple Hannah Montana albums, concerts, DVDs, and a movie.

Hannah Montana lasted four seasons and was a launching pad for Miley Cyrus to continue her work in Hollywood and the music industry.

May 5, 2006

Disney purchases Pixar Animation Studios.

Not even a year on the job, and Robert Iger made a business move that solidified his legacy as president of the Walt Disney Company: he introduced an iconic mouse to a decade-old cowboy.

After the success of *Toy Story*, Pixar and Disney signed an agreement offering a fifty-fifty split of development costs and profits for five full-length movies. The deal was over after the release of *Cars* in 2006. Not willing to lose the valuable commodity that had blossomed into Pixar, Iger knew he needed to secure another deal with the studio. In May of 2006, Iger announced that he had bested his predecessor, Michael Eisner, and flat out acquired Pixar Studios rather than merely signing another partnership deal.[46]

Apparently, Steve Jobs of Pixar and Michael Eisner mixed like oil and water. There were reports back in 2004 that after ten long months of negotiations, Jobs walked away from the negotiating table due to some negativity coming from Eisner. Jobs claimed Eisner made negative remarks about Pixar despite the fact that Pixar had contributed to more than half of the studio's profits for about five years.[47]

In an interview with *Fortune* magazine after Disney acquired Pixar, John Lasseter, the creative mastermind at the studio, elaborated on the dynamic between trying to get a deal done with Eisner versus actually getting a deal done with Iger.

The on-again-off-again discussions with Michael Eisner to get a new deal with Disney had to be the most frustrating negotiation on the planet. We would tell them what we thought was important, and the next thing you know, what we asked for was leaked into the public. And then we had to wait months for them to come back to us with a counterproposal. It was just crazy.

It would have been easier just to walk away, but Steve [Jobs] stayed in there for me because I loved these characters that we have created. They're like family, like children. And if we didn't get a deal, Disney would own our children. Who knew what they would do? These were the people that put out "Cinderella II." We believe that the only reason to do a sequel is if you have a great story, period. It's not "Let's just keep cranking it out."

So we started talking to other studios. This was in January 2004. But later it became clear that Disney's board was getting serious about replacing Michael Eisner, so we decided to wait and see what happened.

As it turned out, I got a call from Bob Iger the day it was announced that he would take over as CEO. And that said a lot to us, because he was serious about wanting to make a deal with us to keep distributing our films. He understood that the biggest issue for us wasn't money, but to have control of our characters.

Bob also realized immediately that Disney's reputation with families had dropped because the stuff they were making wasn't as high quality as it used to be. It was more about quantity, not quality. I'm not exactly sure how the idea of Disney's acquisition of Pixar came up, but at first, I was very nervous.

We have this precious entity that is Pixar. It's like a living organism, like we had found out a way to grow life on a planet that had never supported it before. We wondered if a deal like this would ruin it all. But Steve said to Ed [Catmull, Pixar's founder, and president] and me, "Get to know Bob Iger. That's all I can say. He's a good man."

Bob came up to my home, had dinner with my wife and me, and met my kids. And right away I realized this guy is different. It's not that he was just saying the right things. You could feel that he meant it. I think the simplest thing was that he readily admitted what he didn't know and was comfortable with that. But he said he did know one thing: that animation is the heart, soul, and engine that drives this train called Disney, and that it was broken, and that it needs to be fixed.

He told me his epiphany happened when Hong Kong Disneyland opened last fall, and he was there with his young kids watching the opening-day parade. He was watching all the classic Disney characters go by, and it hit him that there was not one character that Disney had created in the past ten years. Not one. All the new characters were invented by Pixar. That's when he made the decision. I was still nervous about how Pixar was going to change if it became a part of Disney. And Bob simply said, "This is going to be very expensive, so it's in my best interest to do everything I can to keep it the same." He was so calm and logical. No politics, no hidden meaning. And what I realized is that Steve was right about this guy.[46]

And with that, the deal was done. Disney acquired Pixar for $7.4 billion, earning Steve Jobs a seat on Disney's board, along with several billion dollars. As for John Lasseter, everything came full circle for him with this deal when he was named chief creative officer of both studios, reporting solely to Robert Iger.[48]

John had not only been a ride operator at Disneyland, but he had attended the Walt Disney–created art school, Cal Arts. He even worked for the Disney studio from 1979 to 1983 before being fired. Let's have John tell the story of how he got started in animation.

When I was a freshman in high school I read a book about the making of Disney's "Sleeping Beauty" called "The Art of Animation." It was this weird revelation for me, because I hadn't considered that people actually get paid to make cartoons. So I started writing letters to Disney Studios, saying I wanted to be an animator. They were nice and wrote back. Get a great art education, they told me. Learn the basics of figure drawing and design and color, and then we'll teach you animation, because no one teaches that in college.

Then in my senior year, I got a letter from Disney saying they were starting a Character Animation Program at the California Institute of the Arts film school and that it would be taught by these artists from the heyday of Disney. We couldn't quite afford it, but I got a scholarship and enrolled in the very first class.

It was amazing. I had these incredible teachers, and not only were they teaching us great skills, but we were hearing their stories of working with Walt Disney. Walt and these guys took animation from its infancy and created the art form that we know, and now these guys were handing the information to us, this group of unbelievably excited kids.

I finally realized that I wasn't the only one with this geeky love for animation. We could come out of the closet now. And all of us had the same dream: to work at Disney one day. [His classmates included Tim Burton (director of *Corpse Bride* and others), Brad Bird (*The Incredibles*), and John Musker (*Aladdin*).]

I couldn't think of anything better than working at Disneyland during the summer breaks from Cal Arts. At first I was a sweeper in Tomorrowland the summer that Space Mountain opened [1977], and then I transferred to be a ride operator on the Jungle Cruise ride. No one really believes this, but the Jungle Cruise taught me a lot of what I know about comedy and comic timing.

Something just clicked—the combination of having your captive audience in the boat and this script of corny jokes. Soon I learned that the worse the puns and jokes, the funnier they could be, if you knew how to deliver them.

Another key thing that made me who I am happened that same summer. It was the year "Star Wars" came out. I went down opening weekend to Mann's Chinese Theater in Hollywood with a friend from school, and I remember standing in line for about six hours. We finally got inside, and when that movie started, you were swept away. By the end, I was just shaking. I looked around the audience, and it was families, it was teenagers, it was old people—everybody was there, and everybody was just having so much fun.

When Walt Disney was making his films he trusted his instincts and made films for himself, but they appealed to everybody, not just kids. "Snow White," the first full-length animated feature film, was the No. 1 movie in 1938, and it entertained the broadest possible audience. So when I sat there and saw "Star Wars," I was thinking that animation could do this too."[46]

In an effort to shorten the details of John's ascent to the creative king at Disney, let's sprinkle a little Pixar dust again and wrap up the story. John finished his studies at Cal Arts and got a job at the Disney Studios in 1979. He chugged along until 1983, when he was fired.

In 1984, John joined the computer division of Lucasfilm as an interface designer. In 1986, Steve Jobs purchased the division and renamed it Pixar. Three years later, as covered in the decade of the 1980s, Pixar won an Academy Award in 1989, and the rest is computer-generated animation history.[45]

June 29, 2007

Ratatouille is released.

Au revoir, McDonalds! *C'est la vie*, Subway! Disney was going high-brow to promote *Ratatouille*, the Pixar full-length feature about an anthropomorphic rat in Paris who could show Rachel Ray a thing or two in the kitchen.

Bottles of French 2004 vintage white Burgundy were to feature Remy, the little critter that stars in the film. Sounds like a good pairing, right? The movie is set in Paris, Remy the rat cooks French cuisine, and, as Euro Disney told us, the French want their Disney with wine.

Well, not so fast. After some complaints, Disney and Costco, the retailer planning to carry the wine, canceled the promotion before bottles hit the shelves. The label for *Ratatouille* wine had Remy holding a rat-sized glass of wine. Members of the California wine community and opponents of underage drinking claimed that Remy might appeal to those under the legal drinking age, and therefore the promotion should be scraped, which it was.[49]

With or without a wine promotion, Remy did OK at the box office, taking in over $600 million worldwide.[50]

April 14, 2008

Ollie Johnston, the last member of Disney's legendary Nine Old Men, passes away.

Lovers of Disney history, particularly of the animation, are probably familiar with the phrase "Disney's Nine Old Men."

Walt gave this nickname to a group of his most trusted animators, despite the fact that most of them were in their twenties at the time. Walt borrowed the name from President Franklin D. Roosevelt's description of the US Supreme Court's members, who continually squashed many of his New Deal programs.[51]

The illustrious group consisted of Ward Kimball, Eric Larson, Frank Thomas, Marc Davis, Ollie Johnston, Les Clark, Milt Kahl, John Lounsbery, and Woolie Reitherman.

In April of 2008, the last of the "old men" from Disney's golden age, Ollie Johnston, passed away at the age of ninety-five of natural causes.

If you've ever watched *Snow White and the Seven Dwarfs, Fantasia, Bambi, Cinderella, Alice in Wonderland, Peter Pan, Lady and the Tramp, Sleeping Beauty, 101 Dalmatians, Mary Poppins, The Jungle Book, The Aristocats, Robin Hood,* or *The Rescuers,* you've seen some of Ollie's handiwork.

Ollie joined the studio when it was expanding and ramping up production for *Snow White* in the mid-1930s. His salary at the time was seventeen dollars a week.[51]

On *Snow White,* he worked as an assistant animator and then became an animation supervisor on *Fantasia* and *Bambi.* If you're one of the millions of people who get teary-eyed when Bambi's mother gets killed, this scene was something Ollie was very proud of. "The mother's death showed how convincing we could be at presenting really strong emotion."[51]

Ollie became a Disney Legend in 1989, and in 2005, he was the first animator awarded the National Medal of Arts, at a White House ceremony.[51]

October 2008

Disney launches the Disney English learning centers in China.

In 1990, the Walt Disney Company created Disney's American Teacher Awards, which honored outstanding teachers who inspired the joy of learning in America's public- and private-school students in prekindergarten through twelfth grade.[52]

Similar to the Oscars or Grammys, honorees attended an award ceremony that was televised nationally on the Disney Channel. After nearly two decades of celebrating the profession, Disney stopped their award show after the 2006 ceremony.

Two years later, Disney went from honoring the classroom to joining it when they opened their first Disney English learning center in China.

China being the most populous country in the world, it was only natural for Disney to be enticed by the opportunity the country represented. Hong Kong Disneyland had given Disney its first substantial physical presence in the Chinese market in 2005, but Disney always yearned for a physical presence in mainland China, and Disney English was its foray.

Disney opened its first English learning center in Shanghai in 2008. Today their teaching presence has grown to numerous learning centers in Shanghai, Beijing, Guangzhou, Chengdu, Nanjing, Shenzhen, and Suzhou.[53]

The centers teach in an immersive environment where students may become fluent in both English and Disney, as Disney's content, characters, and story lines are utilized during instruction.

The Disney English curriculum consists of three levels: Hello World for ages two and three, Scholars for ages three to six, and Advanced Scholars for ages six to twelve.[53]

Students attend classes a couple of days a week after their traditional schooling. The program costs upward of $2500 for ninety-six hours of class time.[54]

In a society where the government still largely controls the airwaves and presence of foreign media and influence, Disney English is quite an ingenious way to extend the Disney brand and provide a service to the children of China.

March 10, 2009

D23, the official Disney fan club celebrating all things Disney, is launched.

Watch out, Trekkies and Comic-Con visitors. Make way for D23! The disciples of Disney finally have a fan club to call their own.

The *D*, obviously, stands for Disney, and the number 23 represents the year Walt went to Hollywood to start his storied career.

The club has an active presence on the Internet, with their website providing a treasure trove of Disney history and information. But probably best of all about D23 are the fan expo events. This is where fans of Disney can let their freak flag fly and fully submerge themselves in their favorite subculture.

The expo features celebrity appearances, a variety of presentations, and the Disney Legends ceremony. Over the years it has been the setting for Disney to make major announcements regarding their future projects. The inaugural D23 Expo was in September of 2009; subsequent events have taken place biannually.

May 29, 2009

The film *Up* is released.

During the decade of the 2000s, there were so many great movies produced by both Disney and Pixar that the decision to include a film or exclude one from *The Disney Story* was a difficult one. Pixar just kept churning out hit after hit. Honestly, nearly every movie they released is worthy of a spot in the book.

For example, the movie *Cars*, with its sequels and spin-offs, is quite important when chronicling Disney. Yet it isn't included in the book—well, now it sort of is. The film won awards, made lots of money, and warranted a presence in the Disney theme parks—which is common across the Pixar movies.

Commercial success and marketability appear to be in the DNA of the Pixar films. They are well-thought-out, witty, and engaging films. They transcend generations and appeal to young and old alike. And for the movie *Up*, the young-and-old dynamic that plays out on-screen is why it made the cut.

Plenty of Disney and Pixar films have meanings and lessons within the subtext of their stories—often conveyed via monsters, planes, princesses, or toys. This is where *Up* is more complicated and emotional. The film is a serendipitous story about a road trip gone awry with a widowed curmudgeon and an innocent, young boy.

The unlikely bond and dynamic that plays out between the duo is fantastic and engaging, and therein lies the beauty of the film—which is one of the reasons the film was nominated for Oscar's best picture.

But long before Pixar's tenth animated film hit the award circuit, it worked the festival circuit. The esteemed Cannes Film Festival selected *Up* to kick off their festivities, which was a first for an animated film.[55]

Attendees of the Cannes Festival previewed the movie, which had taken the folks at Pixar four years to cultivate. Many involved in the creation of the story had a personal attachment, such as Bob Peterson, *Up*'s codirector and cowriter.

> Carl Fredricksen is based on friends and relatives of the filmmakers. "Up" might well be considered the studio's most personal film. "I think so too," said Bob Peterson, "Up's" co-director and co-writer, who also lends his voice to one of the film's dogs. "It's an homage to our grandparents, and that makes it personal."[55]

And in what is perhaps a fascinating case of life somewhat imitating art, Carl Fredricksen, meet Edith Macefield. In 2006, Edith, an octogenarian, turned down $1 million from developers for her home. Her reason was simple. "I don't want to move. I don't need the money. Money doesn't mean anything."[56]

So Edith stood her ground, and the developers built around her, literally. Cranes were brought in, and construction moved right along around her home—which looked similar to Carl Fredricksen's house in *Up*. She continued to live in her little house on the 1400 block of Northwest Forty-Sixth Street in Seattle, Washington, as concrete walls started to envelop her, mere feet from her windows.

When Edith was asked about the noisy construction going on around her, she gave this laissez-faire response: "I went through World War II; the noise doesn't bother me. They'll get it done someday."[56]

When Disney started to promote *Up* in May of 2009, Edith's story caught their attention. As a promotional stunt, publicists went to her home and tied hundreds of balloons to her house to make it resemble Carl's house in the movie.

Unfortunately, Edith wasn't there to see it. She passed away in 2008, at the age of eighty-six.[57] Look for Edith's house to come to the big screen, as her story is going to be made into a movie.

October 1, 2009

The Walt Disney Family Museum opens in San Francisco, California.

As the headline of her obituary in the *New York Times* proclaimed in November of 2013, Diane Disney Miller was the keeper of her father's flame. That is certainly an honorable title and must have been a formidable task to embrace.[58]

We're all protective and proud of our parents in some aspect. Try to wrap your mind around being Walt Disney's daughter for a minute, standing in that shadow long after the man casting it is gone.

Walt's legacy is prominent and omnipresent around the world. And as ridiculous as this may sound, to many of Disney's biggest fans, the man himself is actually unknown. Could Walt Disney really become forgotten to future generations? As the Walt Disney Company's own research revealed, "Many guests under the age of fifteen do not know Walt was a real person."[59]

> At Orlando's Metro West Elementary School, 62 children in kindergarten, first and second grade were interviewed. About a quarter of their parents work for Disney, yet not one kid knew Walt Disney was an actual man.
>
> Third through fifth graders at Metro West knew a bit more about Walt, but some are already jaded. How should his 100th birthday be celebrated? "Lower ticket prices," suggested Heloisa Oliviera, 10.

Many of the 76 kids interviewed in these upper grades thought
Walt was still alive. "His job is telling Mickey and Minnie what
to do in the shows," said Miles Nelson, eight. "He lives in that
big castle."

Disney died of lung cancer, but only two children knew
that. Some kids assumed, that like other great men he was
assassinated."[59]

Diane was well aware that the lines were blurred between real and fantasy when
it came to her father. In 2001, she made this comment: "They think he's a made
up character like Betty Crocker or Ronald McDonald."[59]

The museum was done elegantly and away from the glimmer of the Disney
theme parks and created without the association of the Walt Disney Company.
The museum takes you on Walt's life journey, from his birth to how the world
reacted to his passing and everything in between.

The forty-thousand-plus-square-feet of all things Walt is a tremendous
testament to the brilliance that was Walt Disney. As the years progressed and
his empire expanded, his name took on a life of its own and is now synonymous
with so many things in entertainment. The museum will remind you that Walt
was merely a man, son, husband, father, grandfather.

By creating the Walt Disney Family Museum in 2009, Diane set out to preserve
and enrich her father's legacy. At the same time, she created a wonderful legacy
of her own, ensuring neither father nor daughter will be forgotten. In short,
the museum is a living testament to Walt's infamous quote "If you can dream
it, you can do it."

December 16, 2009

Roy. E. Disney, son of cofounder Roy O. Disney and nephew of Walt Disney,
passes away.

Where would the world be without Disney? We don't have to ponder that
question, due to the ingenuity of Walt and Roy O. Disney. Perhaps a better
question to propose is, where would Disney be today without Roy E. Disney?

Would the company have been dismantled in 1984 when Mickey and the crew
hit tough times and corporate raiders had a buffet on Disney's stock? The

same question could be asked about the situation in 2004, when Roy E. wanted another change at the top and Comcast was lurking to make an acquisition. Roy E. Disney was a catalyst for two significant changes in the Disney story.

Roy E. Disney dug his heels in twice and created some legendary Disney drama in the name of change. Was it for ego, money, or an honest, deep-rooted feeling that the company needed to forge ahead in a different direction? We will never have the answer to this question. Regardless of where Roy E.'s intentions were rooted, one thing is clear: Disney prospered in the years after he intervened and shaped the company significantly.

Was Roy a knight in shining armor battling to save the Disney kingdom? Well, that analogy may have a bit too much pixie dust sprinkled on it. But Pope John Paul II thought he was pretty special, and in January of 1998, the pope awarded Roy a papal knighthood.[60]

Roy was seventy-nine when he passed away on December 16, 2009. Both his father and uncle died in the month of December as well, Walt on December 15, and Roy O. on December 20.

December 31, 2009

Disney completes their acquisition of Marvel Entertainment.

The next time Buzz Lightyear runs into trouble with Emperor Zurg, maybe he can reach out to Spider-Man or Iron Man for some backup, as they are all now part of the Disney family.

In the summer of 2009, Disney announced their second major acquisition in three years, Marvel Entertainment, for $4 billion.

Disney's purchase of Marvel wasn't as straightforward as their purchase of Pixar.

Despite Marvel's history of licensing out their characters to other studios, Marvel and Disney didn't have a longstanding working relationship like the one Disney had with Pixar.

To accomplish this acquisition, Robert Iger had his work cut out for him. It appears as though Marvel's owner, Isaac Perlmutter, had a superpower of his own: his strong will. Here's a bit about how the purchase went down from the *LA Times*.

To get Marvel, Disney would have to convince owner Isaac Perlmutter, a sharp-elbowed Israeli American businessman, that it was time to sell.

"Ike was difficult to reach, didn't engage very much and never came to Hollywood," Iger said. Iger eventually got on Perlmutter's schedule: They would meet in June 2009 at the inscrutable Marvel executive's offices in Manhattan.

Iger walked into Perlmutter's office by himself and told the story of buying Pixar, hammering on the opportunities it created. Iger also suggested that Perlmutter telephone Jobs, who could share his experience of selling Pixar to Disney.

"I basically tried to convince him that I was a trustworthy guy—not only was my handshake good but I'd be a good steward of his people and the brand," Iger said.

He said that the $4-billion deal was effectively clinched over dinner with their wives at an Upper East Side steakhouse.

Under Disney, Marvel has released three films that have topped $1 billion at the box office: "The Avengers," "Iron Man 3" and "Avengers: Age of Ultron."[61]

Disney was now in possession of some of the world's most famous superheroes, and, as Robert Iger said after the purchase was announced, "This is perfect from a strategic perspective this treasure trove of over 5,000 characters offers Disney the ability to do what we do best."[62]

Bringing Marvel into the Disney fold was certainly a powerful move in Hollywood. They now have several characters to capitalize on within the male demographic, much in the way the company operates their princess franchise.

There is one little snafu with the Marvel deal. Due to preexisting licensing agreements, there would be minimal Marvel exposure within some of the Disney theme parks.

Spiderman made his Disneyland debut in November of 2015, so be sure to soak him up there, as it could be quite some time before he makes his way across the country to Walt Disney World.

As per a licensing agreement Marvel has with Universal Studios (Comcast) theme park in Orlando, Universal owns the exclusive theme park rights for many of Marvel's characters in Florida, which can be seen at their Island of Adventure theme park, across town from WDW.

The way the deal works is; Universal can keep the rights as long as the attractions are in operation, should these attractions close Disney could pounce on the opportunity and capitalize on their characters.[63]

Ok, so it doesn't seem like WDW will be getting a Marvel land anytime soon, but there's always hope for Disneyland!

October 30, 2012

Disney agrees to acquire Lucasfilm, Ltd.

Pixar, Marvel, and now Lucas. During Robert Iger's first seven years running the mouse, he made $16 billion worth of iconic acquisitions.

The tag team of George Lucas and Disney harkens back to the 1980s, when they collaborated on several projects for the Disney theme parks. So it's really no surprise that Disney coveted the works of George Lucas. Lucasfilm, primarily with *Star Wars*, is in a stratosphere of its own in the world of pop culture and entertainment and was an easy way for Disney to compete and stay relevant across many entertainment genres.

So how did Mickey woo Luke Skywalker? Apparently it all came down to a meal again. It seems as though Robert Iger does some of his best work not only in the boardroom but the dining room.

Iger solidified the foundation for the Pixar deal after breaking bread with John Lasseter and his family at John's home. He closed the agreement for Marvel at a steakhouse in New York City, and he made his sales pitch to George Lucas over breakfast at WDW's Brown Derby restaurant at Disney's Hollywood Studios in 2011.[61]

During their meal, Iger spoke about the success of both Pixar and Marvel since Disney had acquired them, leading George Lucas to respond, "If there is anyone I want to sell to, it is you."[61]

Six months later Iger received a phone call from Lucas, who asked if he recalled their breakfast conversation. Lucas was ready to sell, and in October 2012, the deal was announced—$4.06 billion for Lucasfilm Ltd.[61]

In December of 2015, the first installment of a Disney-owned *Star Wars* was released: *Star Wars: The Force Awakens*. The film was a critical success, receiving five Academy Award nominations.

As for the box office returns, just a mere two weeks after its release, the film became the all-time highest-grossing movie in the *Star Wars* franchise. It also holds the record for the fastest film to reach the $500 million mark in America—it took only ten days. Next, it became the fastest film in history to hit the $1 billion mark globally, which only took 12 days.[64]

It sounds as though $4 billion was quite a good deal for Disney. Additional *Star Wars* movies are in the works, as well as the addition of Star Wars Land at Disneyland and Walt Disney World.

November 27, 2013

The movie *Frozen* is released.

When examining the success of Disney's animated features, there are a few necessary attributes that may be used as a barometer. Was it nominated for or win any awards? Did it break box office records? Was there a song that topped the charts and sold millions of albums or downloads? We're talking Disney here, so, of course, there's always a substantial amount of merchandise, so that is moot. And, lastly, will there be an eventual theme park presence and tie-in?

Frozen accomplished all of these benchmarks and added its own twist that overshadows monetary or commercial success. This indicator shows the power the movie had over fans. New parents started naming their children after a few of the film's characters, most notably Elsa.

In the United States during the year 2014, over 1,100 babies were named Elsa. It became the 286th most common girl's name that year. Elsa hasn't cracked the list of the top 500 names since 1917.[65]

In the United Kingdom, the name also became more common, as Elsa moved up 243 slots and settled into 88th place, cracking the top 100 for baby name popularity in the UK.[66]

Frozen's influence isn't exclusive to baby girls; even the men of the film were represented during 2014. There were 132 Hanses, up from the previous year's 98. Sven saw a rise to 55 up from 33. Kristoff became the name for 32 baby boys. Olaf is represented 22 times, and even Oaken, the proprietor of the film's trading post and sauna, most likely inspired the naming of a few bundle of joys, as 2013 and 2014 were the only two years at least 5 babies received this name.[65]

The power of Disney is quite remarkable, especially when it comes to influence over children, particularly young girls. While Anna and Elsa aren't included in the Disney princess franchise per se, the sisters have continued Disney's more recent cause of shedding some of the Disney stereotypes of yesterday.

Disney's tradition of recreating age-old fairy tales, killing off the parents, sprinkling in a few obstacles and a villain, and then having a male hero swoop in and save the day has become a tired story line for many.

The Disney of today is empowering their newer characters, making them more independent and courageous. Finally, the Disney princess becomes a heroine.

In the spring of 2016, Disney announced another independent woman into their lineup, Princess Elena of Avalor. La Princesa Elena is Disney's first princess inspired by Latin cultures.

Instead of being introduced to the world via a new Disney movie, like her peers in the princess club, her royal highness made her debut on the Disney Channel in the summer of 2016.[67]

Princess Elena may be the new addition to the multibillion-dollar Disney princess / Frozen franchises, but she has a long way to go if she wants to catch the current "snow queens" of the genre, Anna and Elsa.

June 16, 2016

Shanghai Disneyland opens.

When Michael Eisner visited China in the fall of 1998, he was impressed by the large number of McDonald's restaurants in the major cities of the country. He remarked to shareholders, "The Chinese people love Mickey no less than Big Mac."[68] Not long after this comment, Disney got to work on Hong Kong Disneyland.

As you well know, after Hong Kong Disneyland, the company created Disney English, which became another great opportunity for the company to expand their presence in China. Finally, in 2010, Disney made a big splash by announcing they were building a theme park in Shanghai, the largest city in China, and, for that matter, the world.

Despite Disney's theme park presence in Hong Kong since 2005, Mickey wasn't always a familiar face to the Chinese. Disney had limited exposure in China during the 1930s—*Snow White and the Seven Dwarfs* had a run in Shanghai in 1938, but as the 1940s progressed, Disney's exposure decreased.[69]

Decades later, the people of China could no longer be denied Mi-lao-shu and Tang-lao-ya (Mickey and Donald in Mandarin). In October of 1986, Michael Eisner announced that every Sunday evening at 6:30 for a half hour, a Disney cartoon would be shown on China Central Television Network.[70]

There was an interesting caveat in the deal between Disney and the government of China. Disney agreed to provide the cartoons free of charge and sought no royalties. Instead, Disney wanted the bootleg Mickeys to stop. The company wanted protection and enforcement of their intellectual property across the country.[70]

Over the next two years, 104 cartoon episodes were shown to the masses. The cartoons had an estimated weekly viewership of 250 million people, or roughly 25 percent of China's population in the mid-1980s.[70]

Through much of the 1990s, Disney had moderate success entertaining the people of China. The Dragon Club was a Disney cartoon series for children that became popular on television. Even *The Lion King* was released in theaters and was a big hit. Then things went awry.

Martin Scorsese made a film about China's oppression of the spiritual leader, the Dalai Lama. The film is called *Kundun*, and Disney backed it, a move that irritated the Chinese government. China implored Disney to pull the plug on the project, something they refused to do, as the film was being distributed in the United States and not China. And with that, China's great wall went up on Disney. The company was banned from the country.[71]

In 1998, Disney said they had learned their lesson and called backing the movie a big mistake. They even brought in a hired hand to get the job done—former secretary of state Henry Kissinger lobbied the Chinese government on behalf of the mouse.[71]

Disney was back in the government's good graces, and their relationship grew over time, gradually allowing a bit more Disney to permeate the country. By 2009 China was ready for an all-out Mickey onslaught, and they approved a deal to bring a Disney theme park to Shanghai.

Fast-forward seven years. On a rainy day in mid-June 2016, after spending $5.5 billion over five years, Disney's twelfth theme park opened its gates.

As Robert Iger said on one of his visits during the soft preview, "East meets West. Past meets future. And anything is possible to those who believe." And Iger should know a thing or two about believing, as the deal to get this park done had been quite an endeavor.[72]

Disney made several concessions they wouldn't usually make to get this deal done. For starters, China wouldn't allow Disney to have their Disney Channel broadcast across the country. This is normally a must-have, as it introduces the country to the brand and is crucial for the marketing pipeline.[71]

Next, they had to concede a few things financially. The government would hold a 57 percent interest in the park. They also wanted 30 percent ownership in the management company that would operate the park, in addition to influence over the price of admission, food served, and which rides would be featured in the park.[71]

To keep the state-owned Shanghai Shendei Group happy, the official name of the organization that would control the park, Disney left Space Mountain, the Jungle Cruise, and It's a Small World on the drawing board.

This move was made to keep the rumblings of cultural imperialism at bay. Without these Disney park mainstays, the Imagineers went into overdrive, creating many exclusive attractions found only in Shanghai—roughly 80 percent of the park's attractions are unique to the park.[71]

Disney felt these changes were a necessary adjustment to their plan to gain access to the roughly 330 million people within a three-hour drive or train ride.[71] The first-year expectations for the park are somewhat modest—eleven million for the first year, and after a few years, the number should double.[71]

Disney received glowing reviews on the aesthetics and creativity of the park—which features the world's largest Disney castle along with six unique lands. And as Robert Iger remarked, the park is "authentically Disney and distinctly Chinese."[71]

Perhaps it is only fitting that the final milestone in *The Disney Story* is about a theme park. The Disney parks mean many things to many people, maybe more so than anything else Disney creates.

Annually, over 100 million people seek the escapism and refuge their parks provide. Young and old, wealthy and poor, the company resonates with folks around the globe. For many, the trip to Disney has become a rite of passage.

The Walt Disney Company allows us to make memories unmatched by any other corporate entity in existence. Disney provides the setting for celebrating life's events—honeymoons, marriages, birthdays, and anniversaries. You name it, and surely someone has marked it with a Disney trip.

On these trips, we're fully immersed in their subculture, which in many ways is more impactful than merely creating an experimental prototypical community of tomorrow. We sleep in our Disney beds, eat our Disney food, wear our Disney clothing, watch our Disney TV, and sing our Disney songs, aided by people who make their living from Disney. There are even some folks who never leave a Disney world, as they live in their Disney homes at Golden Oak, just outside of the Magic Kingdom in WDW.

If you're a cynic or a person who believes Disney at its core is nothing more than consumerism, millions of people around the world will tell you otherwise. Quite frankly, for them it really doesn't matter. It's not that deep; it is about forgetting today and living in a fantasy, even if for only a few hours. Your hosts on these escapes are Mickey Mouse and Walt Disney, two of the most transcending figures in the world. Even societies that detest America or American culture are smitten with Disney.

We saw this in 1959 when Nikita Khrushchev threw a fit when he was denied entry to Disneyland, and today when both North Korea and Hamas, utilize bootleg Disney characters in their television broadcasts.[72]

At one point during this story, I remarked that Disney is the world's largest purveyor of nostalgia. In reality, they actually may be the world's largest purveyor of popular culture, something that would most likely make the company's namesake and founder very proud.

Judging by his body of work, Walt loved history, culture, and America—and it is very evident that America (and the world) loves him back. The simple five-letter word, a family's last name, has grown quite powerful. It transcends, unites, educates, and, in its simplest form, brings happiness and joy.

The End—for now!

HERE ARE A FEW MORE IMPORTANT DATES FROM THE 2000S:

January 1, 2000

Fantasia 2000 is released in IMAX theaters.

April 16, 2001

Disney's Animal Kingdom Lodge opens at WDW.

October 24, 2001

Disney acquires the Fox Family Channel and renames it ABC Family Channel.

June 21, 2002

Lilo and Stitch is released in theaters.

May 22, 2003

Disney sells the Anaheim Angels professional baseball team.

May 30, 2003

Finding Nemo is released.

April 2004

Disney acquires Jim Hensen's Muppets.

November 5, 2004

The Incredibles is released.

February 25, 2005

Disney sells the Mighty Ducks professional hockey team.

November 4, 2005

Chicken Little is released.

December 9, 2005

The Chronicles of Narnia: The Lion, the Witch and the Wardrobe is released.

July 7, 2006

Pirates of the Caribbean: Dead Man's Chest is released.

June 11, 2007

Finding Nemo Submarine Voyage opens at Disneyland.

August 17, 2007

High School Musical 2 premiered on the Disney Channel.

November 21, 2007

Enchanted is released.

January 7, 2008

Disney-MGM Studios at Walt Disney World is renamed Disney's Hollywood Studios.

February 1, 2008

Phineas and Ferb debuts on the Disney Channel.

October 28, 2008

Tinker Bell is released.

February 13, 2009

Disney XD launches on cable television.

April 22, 2009

Disneynature releases *Earth*.

August 4, 2009

Bay Lake Tower opens at Walt Disney World's Contemporary Resort.

December 11, 2o09

The Princess and the Frog is released.

March 5, 2010

Alice in Wonderland is released.

June 18, 2o10

Toy Story 3 is released.

November 24, 2010

Tangled is released.

May 20, 2011

Pirates of the Caribbean: On Stranger Tides is released.

June 24, 2011

Cars 2 is released.

August 29, 2011

Disney's Hawaiian resort Aulani opens.

March 23, 2012

Disney Junior premieres on cable television.

May 4, 2012

Marvel's *The Avengers* is released.

June 22, 2012

Brave is released.

November 2, 2012

Wreck-It Ralph is released.

June 21, 2013

Monsters University is released.

August 9, 2013

Planes is released.

December 13, 2013

Saving Mr. Banks is released.

March 21, 2014

Muppets Most Wanted is released.

May 30, 2014

Maleficent is released.

November 7, 2014

Big Hero Six is released.

June 19, 2015

Inside Out is released.

July 17, 2015

Disneyland celebrates its sixtieth anniversary.

June 17, 2016

Finding Dory is released.

END NOTES

As mentioned in the book's introduction and a few times throughout the book, the endnotes from each chapter can be found at thedisneystory.com.

The website is an interactive bibliography. Every article used to create this book is posted in its entirety for your reading enjoyment. Just click on the appropriate chapter and have at it!

CPSIA information can be obtained
at www.ICGtesting.com
Printed in the USA
LVOW07s1447131117
556108LV00040B/2592/P